Contents

What's Great About This Book

Centers are a wonderful, fun way for students to practice important skills. The 13 centers in this book are self-contained and portable. Students may work at a desk, table, or even on the floor. Once you've made the centers, they're ready to use any time.

What's in This Book

The teacher direction page includes how to make the center and a description of the student task.

Full-color materials needed for the center

Reproducible record sheets

Self-checking answer keys

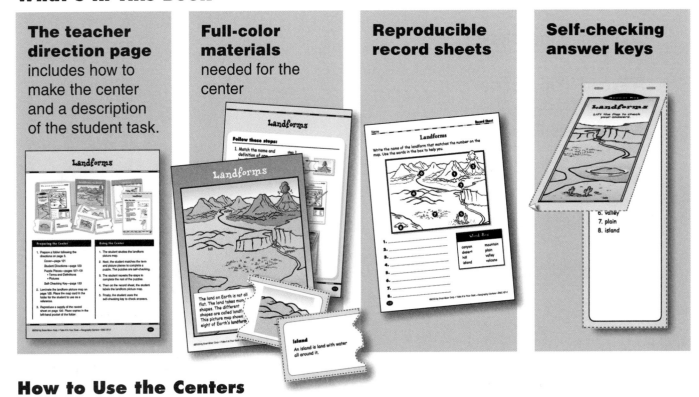

How to Use the Centers

The centers are intended for skill practice, not to introduce skills. It is important to model the use of each center before students do the task independently.

Questions to Consider:

- Will students select a center, or will you assign the centers?
- Will there be a specific block of time for centers, or will the centers be used throughout the day?
- Where will you place the centers for easy access by students?
- What procedure will students use when they need help with the center tasks?
- Where will students store completed work?
- How will you track the tasks and centers completed by each student?

Making a File Folder Center

Folder centers are easily stored in a box or file crate. Students take a folder to their desks to complete the task.

Materials

- folder with pockets
- envelopes
- marking pens and pencils
- scissors
- stapler
- two-sided tape

Steps to Follow

1. Laminate the cover. Tape it to the front of the folder.

2. Laminate the student direction page. Tape it to the back of the folder.

3. Laminate the self-checking answer key(s) for each center. Cut the page in half. Staple the cover on top of the answer key. Place the answer key in the left-hand pocket.

4. Place record sheets, writing paper, and any other supplies in the left-hand pocket.

5. Laminate the task cards. Place each set of task cards in an envelope. Place the labeled envelopes in the right-hand pocket.

6. If needed for the center, tape the sorting mat together. Laminate it and fold in half before placing it in the right-hand pocket of the folder.

Center Checklist

Student Names

Centers

Looking at the Globe										
A World Map Puzzle										
A Compass Rose										
A Map Key										
The United States										
A Map Grid										
Parts of a Map										
Reading a Road Map										
Landforms										
Florida's Waterways										
A Trip to California										
Famous Monuments										
North America										

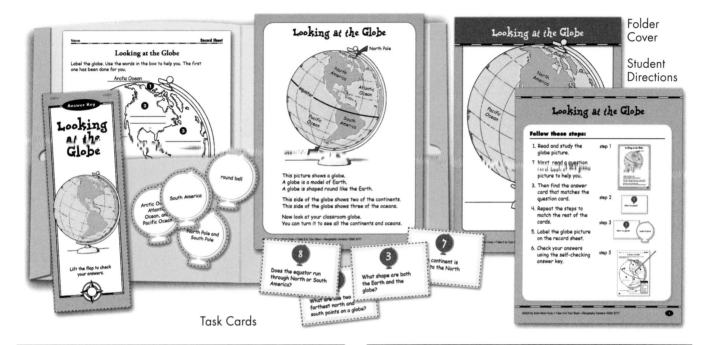

Folder Cover

Student Directions

Task Cards

Preparing the Center

1. Prepare a folder following the directions on page 3.

   Cover—page 7

   Student Directions—page 9

   Task Cards—pages 13 and 15
   • Question Cards—yellow
   • Answer Cards—blue

   Self-Checking Key—page 17

2. Laminate the globe picture on page 11. Place the map card in the folder for student reference.

3. Reproduce a supply of the record sheet on page 6. Place copies in the left-hand pocket of the folder.

4. Provide a classroom globe for student reference.

Using the Center

1. The student reads and studies the globe picture.

2. Next, the student reads and matches the question cards with the answer cards. The cards are self-checking.

3. Then the student labels the globe on the record sheet.

4. The student uses the self-checking key to check answers.

Looking at the Globe

Label the globe. Use the words in the box to help you. The first one has been done for you.

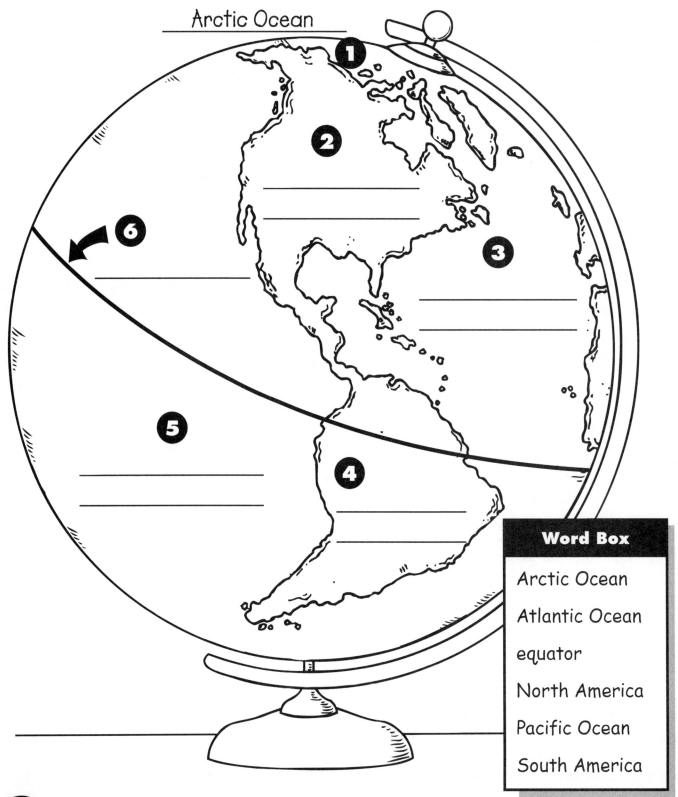

Arctic Ocean

Word Box

Arctic Ocean

Atlantic Ocean

equator

North America

Pacific Ocean

South America

A World Map Puzzle

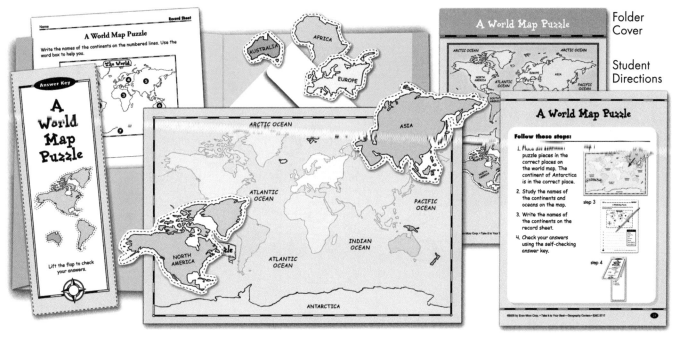

Sorting Mat and Puzzle Pieces

Preparing the Center

1. Prepare a folder following the directions on page 3.

   Cover—page 21

   Student Directions—page 23

   Sorting Mat—pages 25 and 27

   Continent Puzzle Pieces— pages 29 and 31

   Self-Checking Key—page 33

2. Reproduce a supply of the record sheet on page 20. Place copies in the left-hand pocket of the folder.

Using the Center

1. The student places the continent puzzle pieces in the correct places on the sorting mat.

2. Then the student writes the names of the continents on the record sheet.

3. Finally, the student uses the self-checking key to check answers.

A World Map Puzzle

Write the names of the continents on the numbered lines. Use the word box to help you.

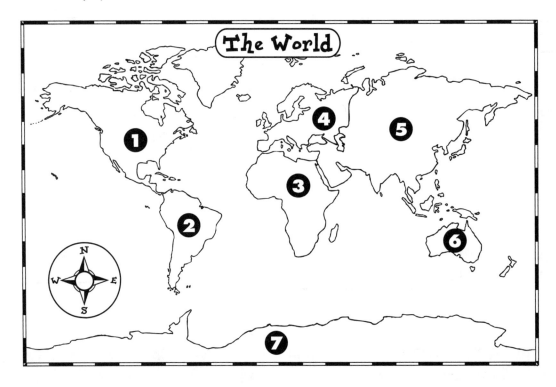

1. _____

2. _____

3. _____

4. _____

5. _____

6. _____

7. _____

Word Box

Africa

Antarctica

Asia

Australia

Europe

North America

South America

A World Map Puzzle

A World Map Puzzle

Follow these steps:

1. Place the six continent puzzle pieces in the correct places on the world map. The continent of Antarctica is in the correct place.

2. Study the names of the continents and oceans on the map.

3. Write the names of the continents on the record sheet.

4. Check your answers using the self-checking answer key.

step 1

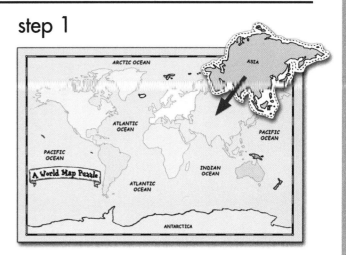

step 3

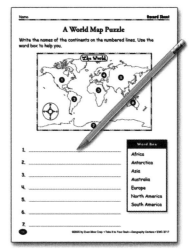

step 4

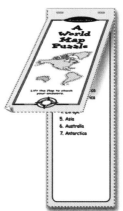

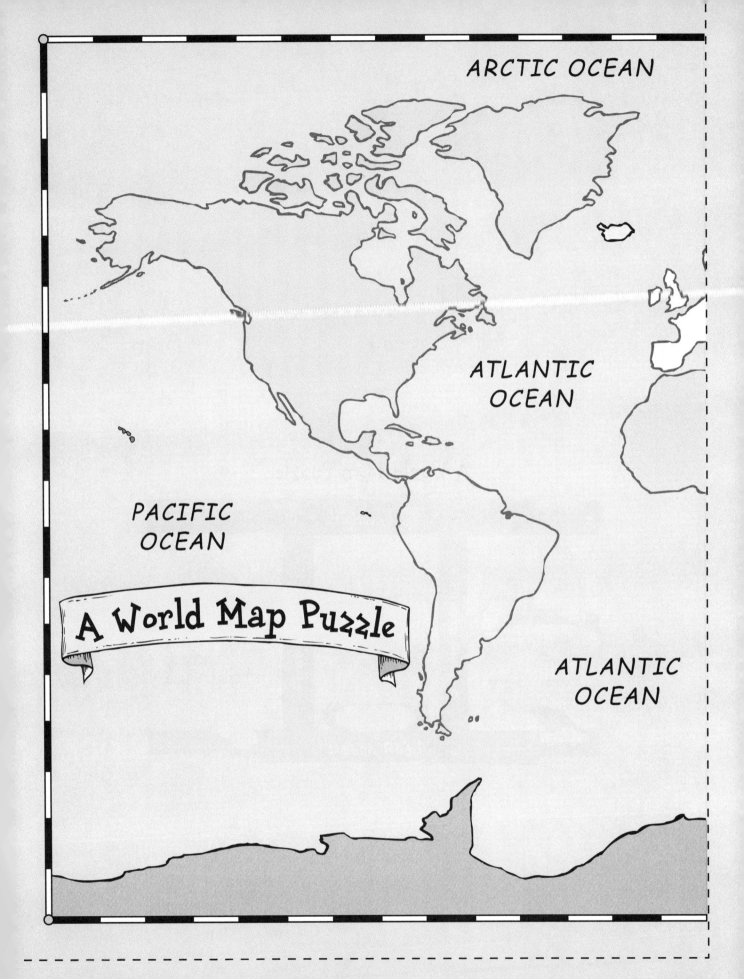

ARCTIC OCEAN

ATLANTIC
OCEAN

PACIFIC
OCEAN

A World Map Puzzle

ATLANTIC
OCEAN

A World Map Puzzle

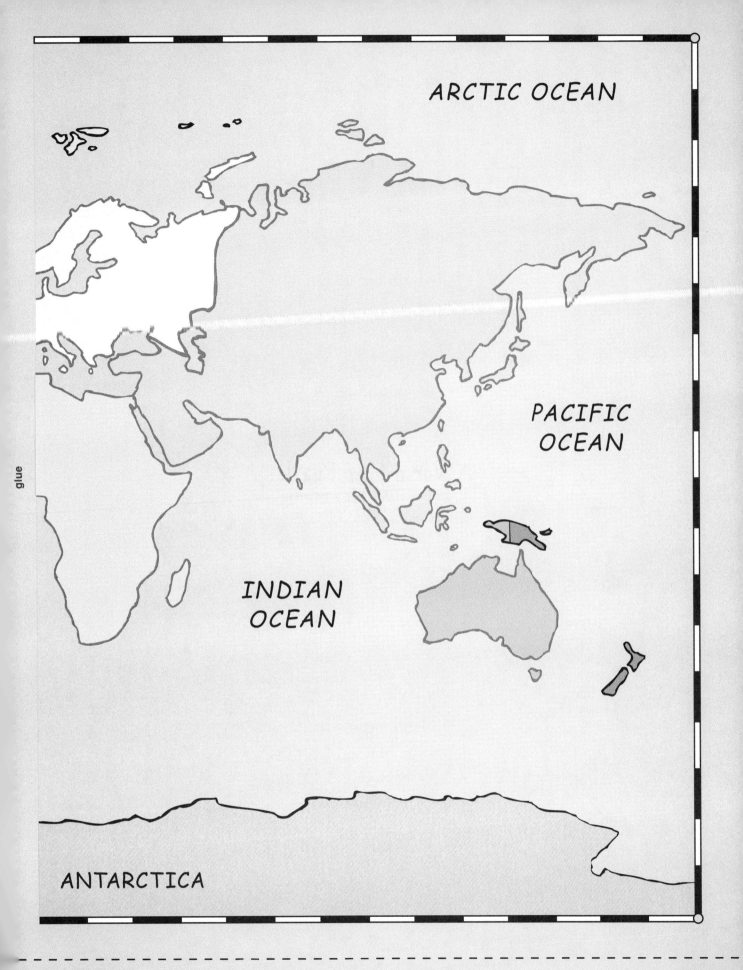

ARCTIC OCEAN

PACIFIC
OCEAN

glue

INDIAN
OCEAN

ANTARCTICA

A World Map Puzzle

©2005 by Evan-Moor Corp. • EMC 3717

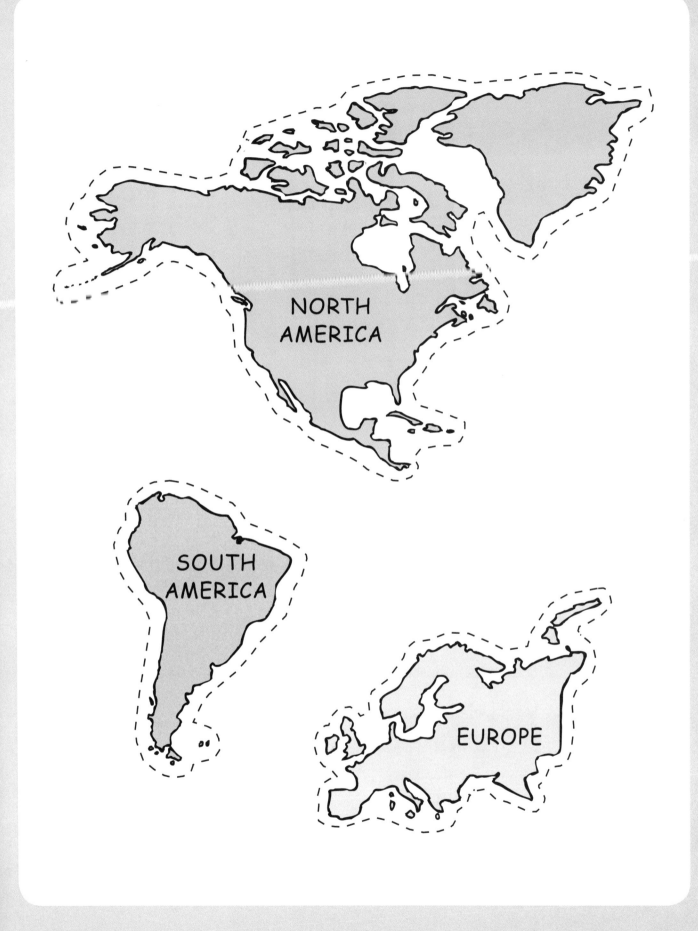

NORTH
AMERICA

SOUTH
AMERICA

EUROPE

A World Map Puzzle

©2005 by Evan-Moor Corp.
EMC 3717

A World Map Puzzle

©2005 by Evan-Moor Corp.
EMC 3717

A World Map Puzzle

©2005 by Evan-Moor Corp.
EMC 3717

ASIA

AUSTRALIA

AFRICA

A World Map Puzzle

©2005 by Evan-Moor Corp.
EMC 3717

A World Map Puzzle

©2005 by Evan-Moor Corp.
EMC 3717

A World Map
Puzzle

©2005 by Evan-Moor Corp.
EMC 3717

A World Map Puzzle

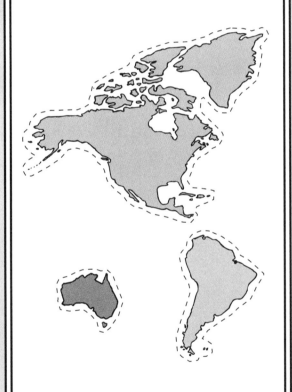

Lift the flap to check
your answers.

A World Map Puzzle

1. North America
2. South America
3. Africa
4. Europe
5. Asia
6. Australia
7. Antarctica

N

W

S

E

A World Map Puzzle

©2005 by Evan-Moor Corp. • EMC 3717

A World Map Puzzle

©2005 by Evan-Moor Corp. • EMC 3717

S

N

W

A Compass Rose

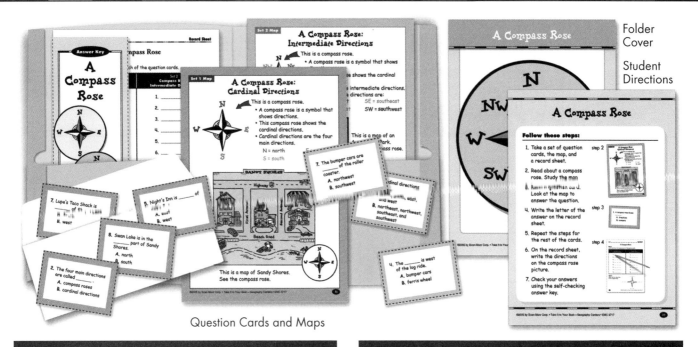

Question Cards and Maps

Folder Cover

Student Directions

Preparing the Center

1. Prepare a folder following the directions on page 3.

   Cover—page 37

   Student Directions—page 39

   Question Cards—pages 43 and 45
   • Set 1—blue
   • Set 2—green

   Self-Checking Key—page 47

2. Laminate the maps on pages 41 and 42. Place the two-sided map card in the right-hand side of the folder for the student to use with the question cards.

3. Reproduce a supply of the record sheet on page 36. Place copies in the left-hand pocket of the folder.

Using the Center

1. The student takes a set of question cards, the matching map, and a record sheet.

2. The student reads about a compass rose and studies the map.

3. Next, the student reads a question card.

4. Then the student records the answer in the correct column on the record sheet.

5. The student repeats the steps for the remaining cards.

6. On the record sheet, the student also completes the compass rose.

7. Finally, the student uses the self-checking key to check answers.

A Compass Rose

Part 1

Write the letter that answers each of the question cards.

Set 1 **Compass Rose: Cardinal Directions**	Set 2 **Compass Rose: Intermediate Directions**
1. _____	1. _____
2. _____	2. _____
3. _____	3. _____
4. _____	4. _____
5. _____	5. _____
6. _____	6. _____
7. _____	7. _____
8. _____	8. _____

Part 2

Write the four directions
on the compass rose.

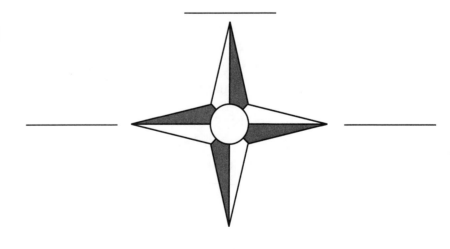

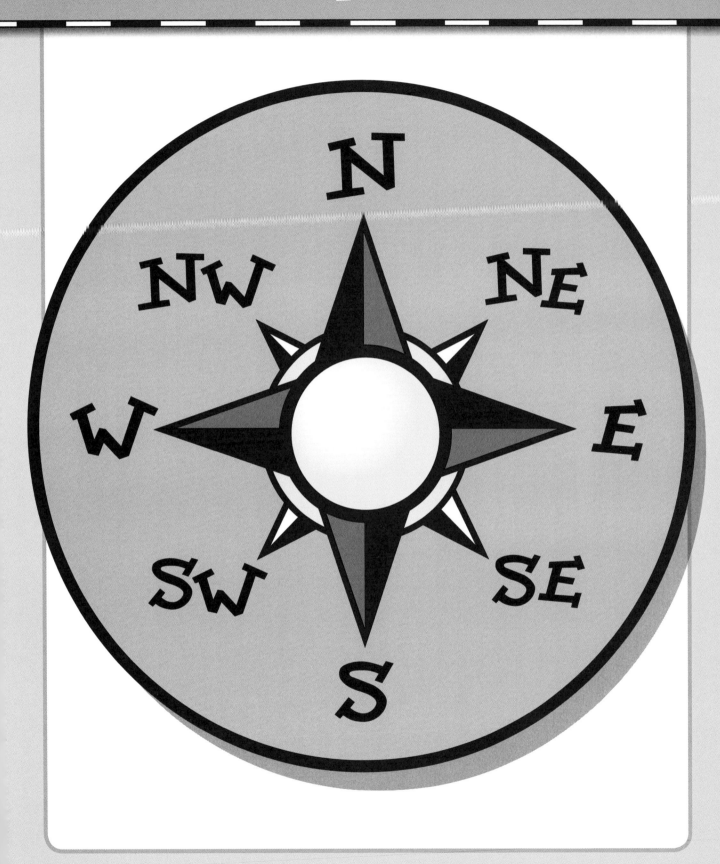

A Compass Rose

Follow these steps:

1. Take a set of question cards, the map, and a record sheet.

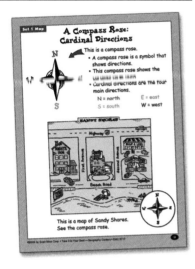

step 2

2. Turn the map to the correct side. Read about a compass rose. Study the map.

3. Read a question card. Look at the map to answer the question.

step 3

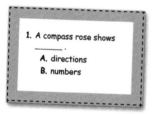

4. Write the letter of the answer in the correct column on the record sheet.

5. Repeat the steps for the rest of the cards.

step 4

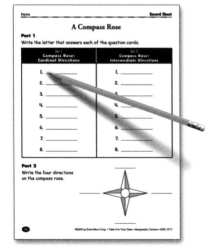

6. On the record sheet, write the directions on the compass rose picture.

7. Check your answers using the self-checking answer key.

A Compass Rose: Cardinal Directions

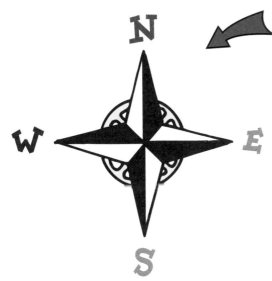

This is a compass rose.

- A compass rose is a symbol that shows directions.
- This compass rose shows the cardinal directions.
- Cardinal directions are the four main directions.

N = north	E = east
S = south	W = west

This is a map of Sandy Shores.
See the compass rose.

A Compass Rose: Intermediate Directions

This is a compass rose.

- A compass rose is a symbol that shows directions.
- This compass rose shows the cardinal directions.
- It also shows the intermediate directions.
- The intermediate directions are:

NE = **northeast**	SE = southeast
NW = northwest	SW = **southwest**

This is a map of an Amusement Park.
See the compass rose.

1. A compass rose shows
   _____ .
   A. directions
   B. numbers

2. The four main directions
   are called _____ .
   A. compass roses
   B. cardinal directions

3. _____ points up on
   a compass rose.
   A. East
   B. North

4. Highway 68 is _____ of
   Beach Road.
   A. north
   B. south

5. Night's Inn is _____ of
   Joe's Gas.
   A. east
   B. west

6. Beach Road runs _____ .
   A. east and west
   B. north and south

7. Lupe's Taco Shack is
   _____ of Shop 4 Less.
   A. south
   B. west

8. Swan Lake is in the
   _____ part of Sandy
   Shores.
   A. north
   B. south

A Compass Rose
Set 1

A Compass Rose
Set 1

A Compass Rose
Set 1

A Compass Rose
Set 1

A Compass Rose
Set 1

A Compass Rose
Set 1

A Compass Rose
Set 1

A Compass Rose
Set 1

1. The cardinal directions are _____ .

    A. north, south, east, and west

    B. northeast, northwest, southeast, and southwest

5. The roller coaster is _____ of the restrooms.

    A. east

    B. southeast

2. The intermediate directions are _____ .

    A. north, south, east, and west

    B. northeast, northwest, southeast, and southwest

6. The merry-go-round is _____ of the log ride.

    A. southeast

    B. southwest

3. NE is between _____ .

    A. north and east

    B. north and west

7. The bumper cars are _____ of the roller coaster.

    A. northwest

    B. southwest

4. The _____ is west of the log ride.

    A. bumper cars

    B. Ferris wheel

8. The _____ is in the southeast part of the park.

    A. gift shop

    B. log ride

A Compass Rose
Set 2
©2005 by Evan-Moor Corp. • EMC 3717

A Compass Rose
Set 2
©2005 by Evan-Moor Corp. • EMC 3717

A Compass Rose
Set 2
©2005 by Evan-Moor Corp. • EMC 3717

A Compass Rose
Set 2
©2005 by Evan-Moor Corp. • EMC 3717

A Compass Rose
Set 2
©2005 by Evan-Moor Corp. • EMC 3717

A Compass Rose
Set 2
©2005 by Evan-Moor Corp. • EMC 3717

A Compass Rose
Set 2
©2005 by Evan-Moor Corp. • EMC 3717

A Compass Rose
Set 2
©2005 by Evan-Moor Corp. • EMC 3717

A Compass Rose

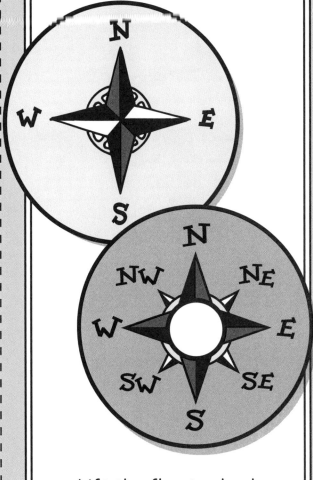

Lift the flap to check your answers.

A Compass Rose

Part 1

Set 1	Set 2
1. A	1. A
2. B	2. B
3. B	3. A
4. A	4. B
5. B	5. A
6. A	6. B
7. A	7. B
8. B	8. A

Part 2

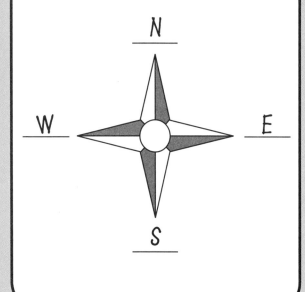

A Compass Rose

A Compass Rose

A Map Key

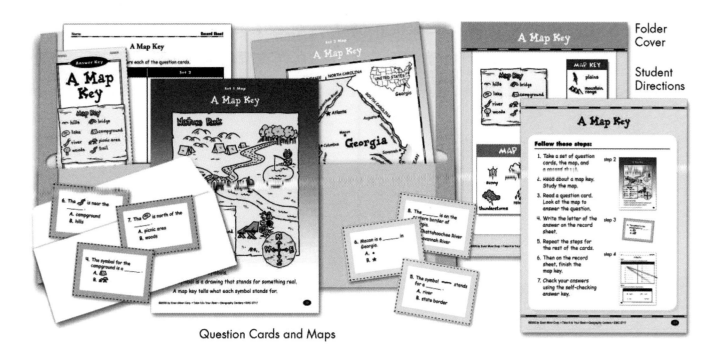

Question Cards and Maps

Folder Cover

Student Directions

Preparing the Center

1. Prepare a folder following the directions on page 3.

   Cover—page 51

   Student Directions—page 53

   Question Cards—pages 57 and 59
   • Set 1—purple
   • Set 2—green

   Self-Checking Key—page 61

2. Laminate the maps on pages 55 and 56. Place the two-sided map card in the right-hand pocket of the folder for the student to use with the question cards.

3. Reproduce a supply of the record sheet on page 50. Place copies in the left-hand pocket of the folder.

Using the Center

1. The student takes a set of question cards, the matching map, and a record sheet.

2. The student reads about a map key and studies the map.

3. Next, the student reads a question card.

4. Then the student records the answer in the correct column on the record sheet.

5. The student repeats the steps for the remaining cards.

6. On the record sheet, the student also draws a symbol on the map key.

7. Finally, the student uses the self-checking key to check answers.

A Map Key

Part 1

Write the letter that answers each of the question cards.

Set 1	Set 2
1. _____	1. _____
2. _____	2. _____
3. _____	3. _____
4. _____	4. _____
5. _____	5. _____
6. _____	6. _____
7. _____	7. _____
8. _____	8. _____

Part 2

Draw a symbol on the map key to show mountains.

Map Key

★ capital   〜〜 river

• city   mountain

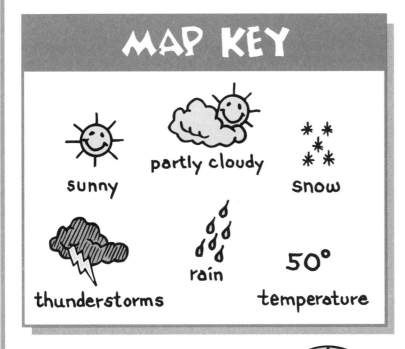

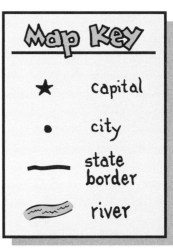

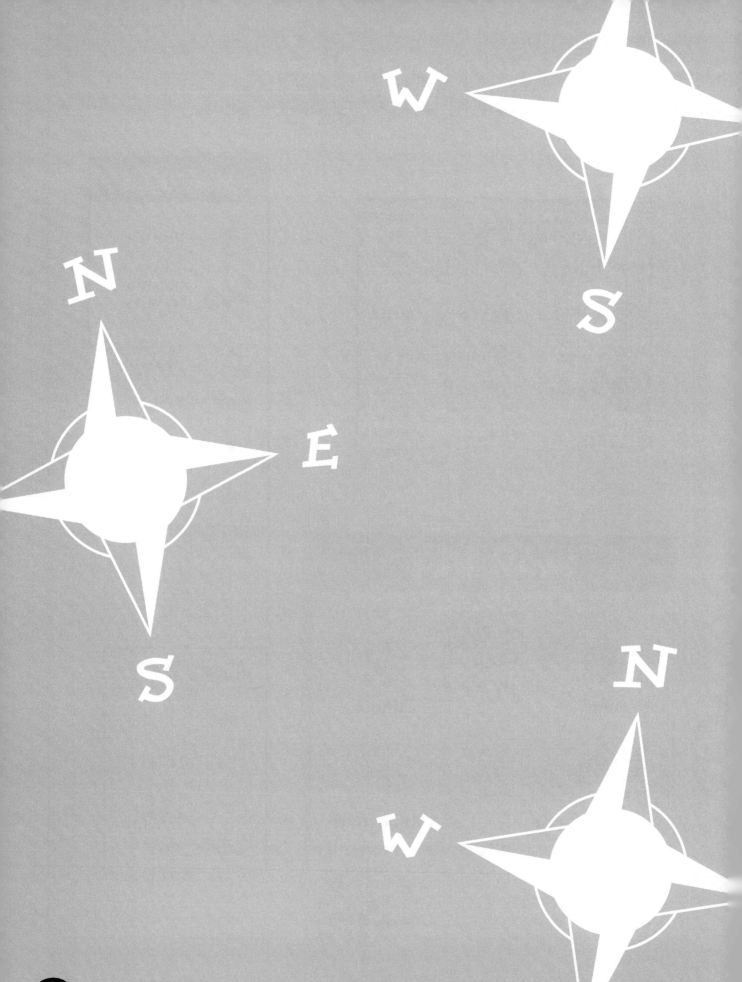

A Map Key

Follow these steps:

1. Take a set of question cards, the map, and a record sheet.

2. Turn the map to the correct side. Read about a map key. Study the map.

3. Read a question card. Look at the map to answer the question.

4. Write the letter of the answer on the record sheet.

5. Repeat the steps for the rest of the cards.

6. On the record sheet, finish the map key.

7. Check your answers using the self-checking answer key.

step 2

step 3

step 4

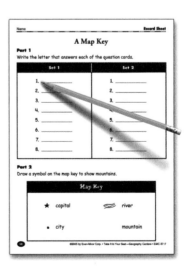

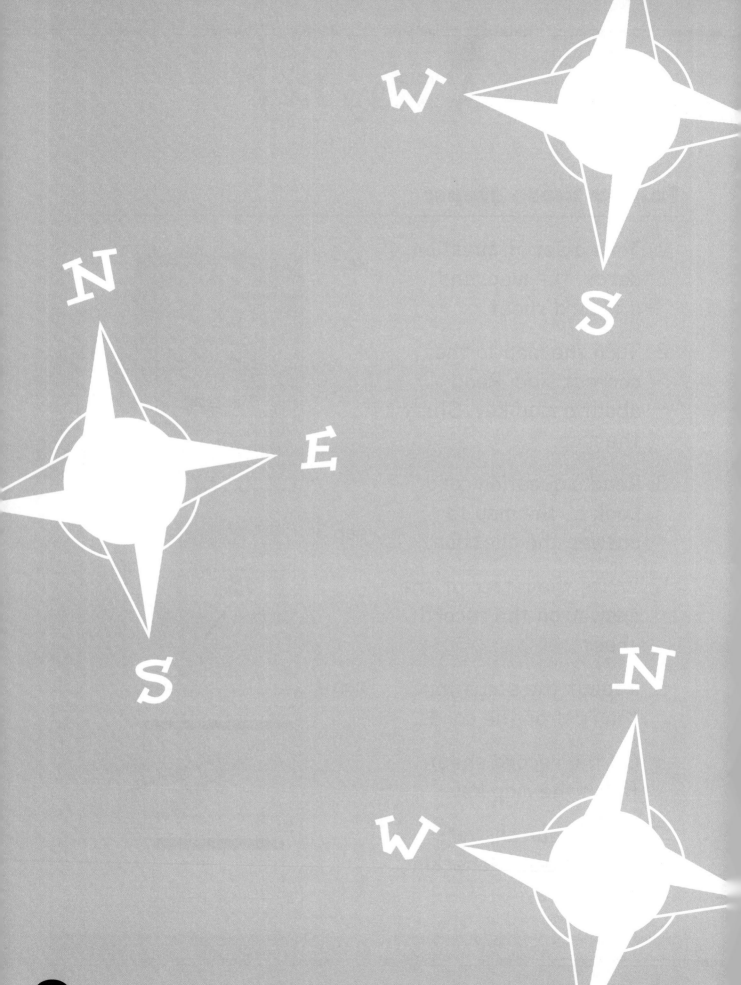

The United States

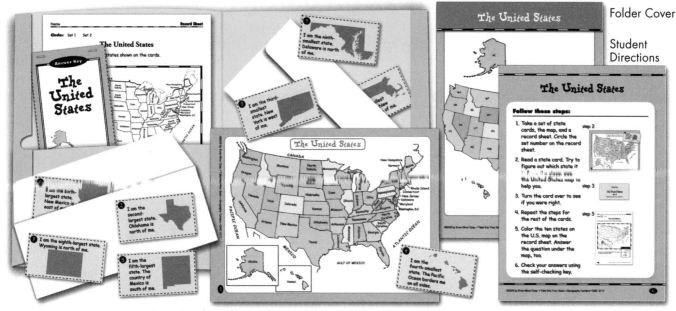

Folder Cover

Student Directions

State Cards and United States Map

Preparing the Center

1. Prepare a folder following the directions on page 3.

    Cover—page 65

    Student Directions—page 67

    State Cards—pages 71 and 73
    • Set 1—pink
    • Set 2—blue

    Self-Checking Key—page 75

2. Laminate the United States map on page 69. Place the map in the right-hand pocket of the folder for the student to use with the state cards.

3. Reproduce a supply of the record sheet on page 64. Place copies in the left-hand pocket of the folder.

Using the Center

1. The student takes a set of state cards, the map, and a record sheet. The student circles the set number on the record sheet.

2. The student takes a state card and the United States map. The student reads the clues and looks at the shape of the state.

3. Next, the student turns the card over to read the name of the state.

4. The student repeats the steps for the remaining cards.

5. The student colors the ten states on the record sheet. The student also answers the question under the map.

6. Finally, the student uses the self-checking key to check answers.

Circle: Set 1   Set 2

The United States

On this map, color the ten states shown on the cards.

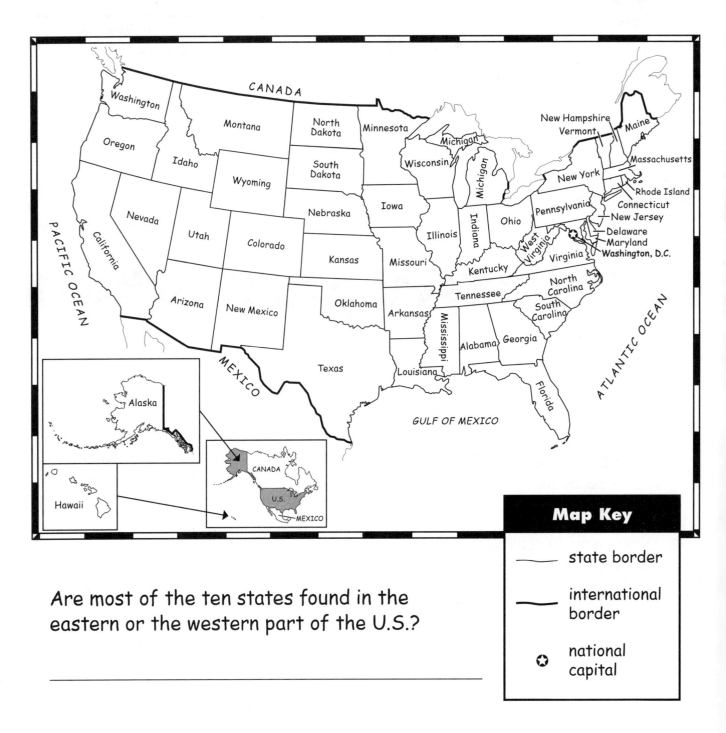

Are most of the ten states found in the eastern or the western part of the U.S.?

_____

Map Key

——— state border

—— international border

⊕ national capital

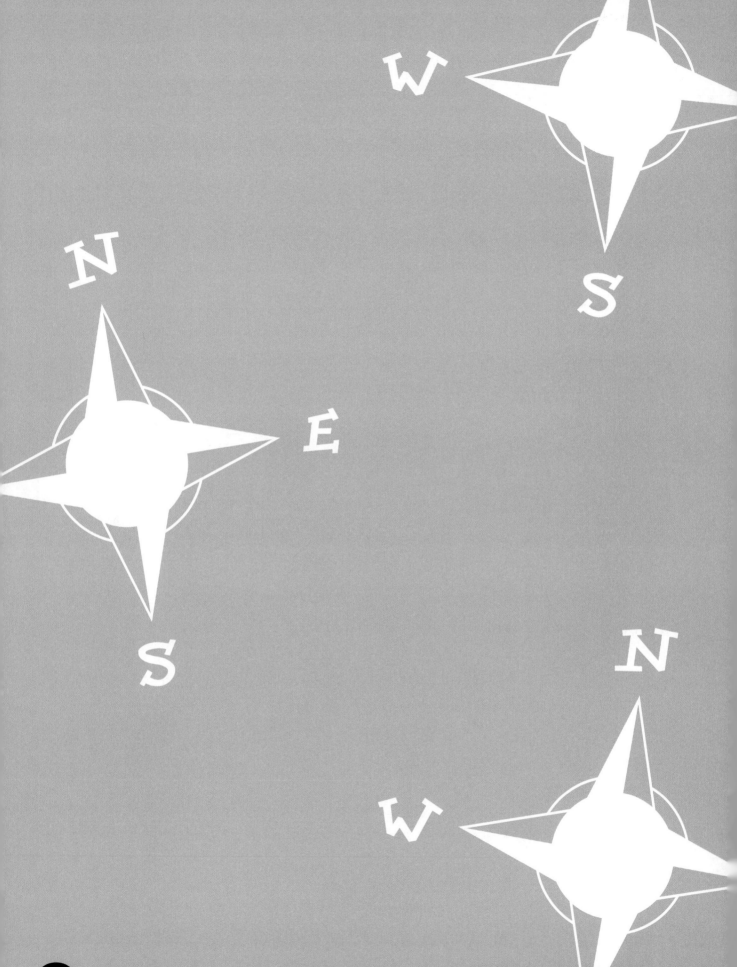

The United States

Follow these steps:

1. Take a set of state cards, the map, and a record sheet. Circle the set number on the record sheet.

2. Read a state card. Try to figure out which state it is from the clues. Use the United States map to help you.

3. Turn the card over to see if you were right.

4. Repeat the steps for the rest of the cards.

5. Color the ten states on the U.S. map on the record sheet. Answer the question under the map, too.

6. Check your answers using the self-checking key.

step 2

step 3

step 5

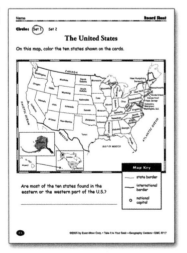

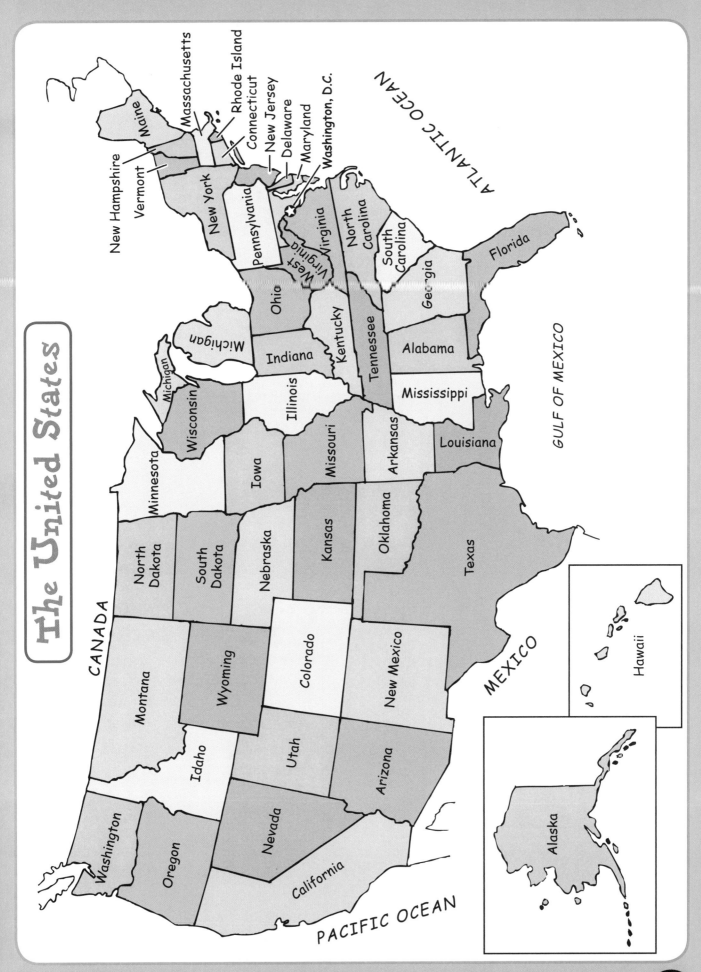

The United States

Massachusetts
Rhode Island
Connecticut
New Jersey
Delaware
Maryland
Washington, D.C.
New Hampshire
Vermont
Maine

ATLANTIC OCEAN

New York
Pennsylvania
West Virginia
Virginia
North Carolina
South Carolina
Georgia
Florida

Ohio
Kentucky
Tennessee
Alabama
Michigan
Indiana
Mississippi

GULF OF MEXICO

Michigan
Wisconsin
Illinois
Missouri
Arkansas
Louisiana

Minnesota
Iowa

North Dakota
South Dakota
Nebraska
Kansas
Oklahoma
Texas

CANADA

Montana
Wyoming
Colorado
New Mexico

Idaho
Utah
Arizona

MEXICO

Washington
Oregon
Nevada
California

Hawaii

Alaska

PACIFIC OCEAN

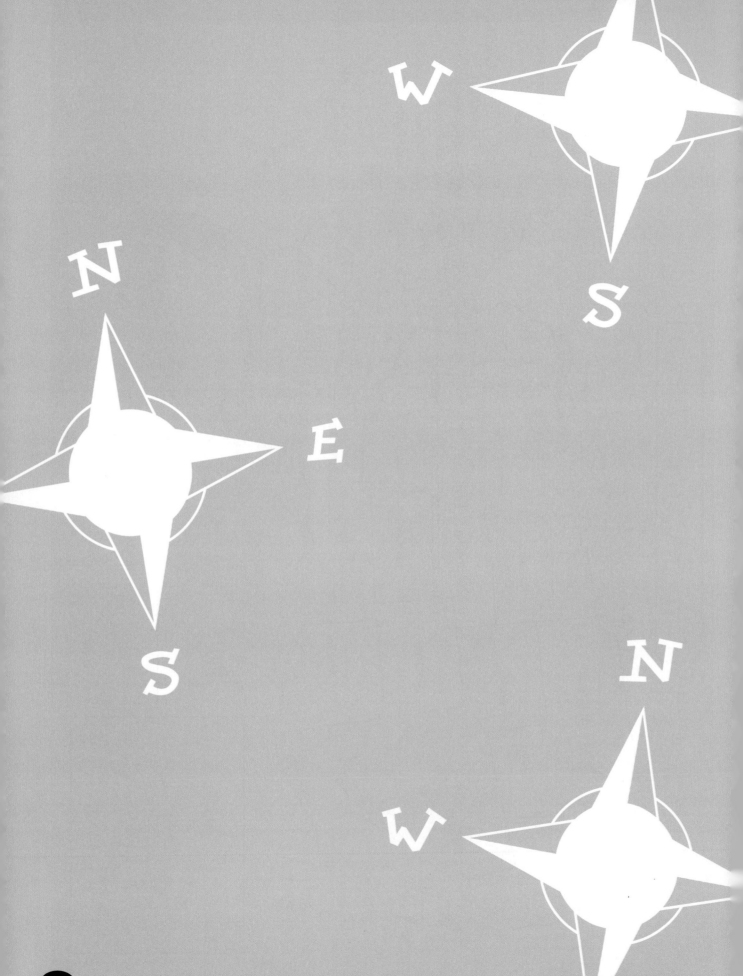

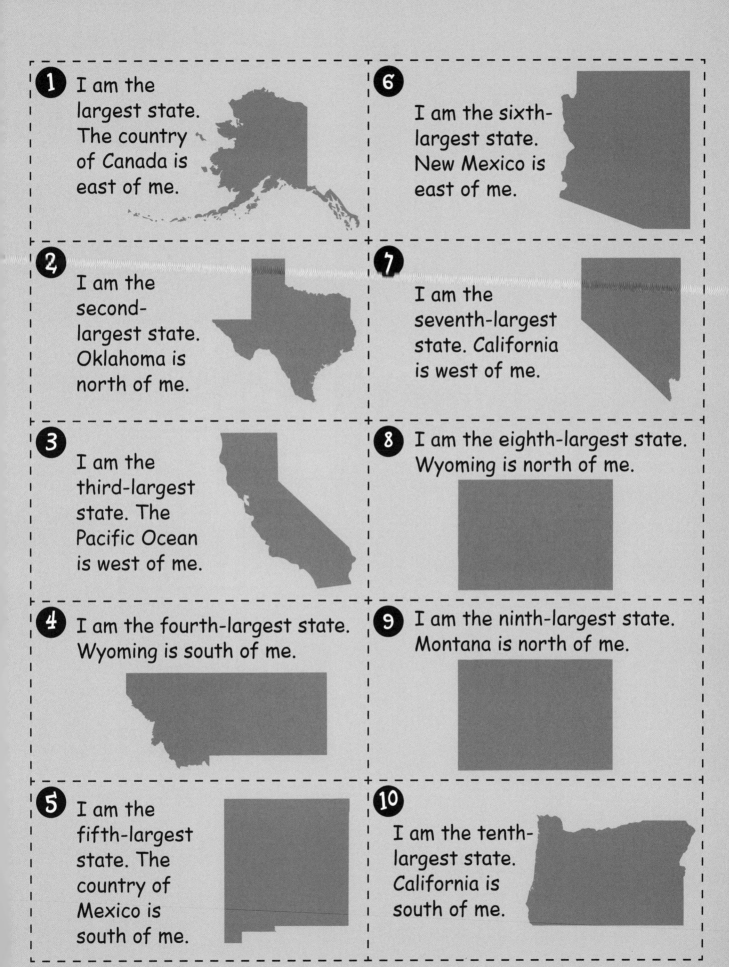

1 I am the largest state. The country of Canada is east of me.

2 I am the second-largest state. Oklahoma is north of me.

3 I am the third-largest state. The Pacific Ocean is west of me.

4 I am the fourth-largest state. Wyoming is south of me.

5 I am the fifth-largest state. The country of Mexico is south of me.

6 I am the sixth-largest state. New Mexico is east of me.

7 I am the seventh-largest state. California is west of me.

8 I am the eighth-largest state. Wyoming is north of me.

9 I am the ninth-largest state. Montana is north of me.

10 I am the tenth-largest state. California is south of me.

Arizona

The United States

Set 1

©2005 by Evan-Moor Corp. • EMC 3717

Alaska

The United States

Set 1

©2005 by Evan-Moor Corp. • EMC 3717

Nevada

The United States

Set 1

©2005 by Evan-Moor Corp. • EMC 3717

Texas

The United States

Set 1

©2005 by Evan-Moor Corp. • EMC 3717

Colorado

The United States

Set 1

©2005 by Evan-Moor Corp. • EMC 3717

California

The United States

Set 1

©2005 by Evan-Moor Corp. • EMC 3717

Wyoming

The United States

Set 1

©2005 by Evan-Moor Corp. • EMC 3717

Montana

The United States

Set 1

©2005 by Evan-Moor Corp. • EMC 3717

Oregon

The United States

Set 1

©2005 by Evan-Moor Corp. • EMC 3717

New Mexico

The United States

Set 1

©2005 by Evan-Moor Corp. • EMC 3717

1 I am the smallest state. Massachusetts is north of me.

2 I am the second smallest state. Pennsylvania is north of me.

3 I am the third-smallest state. New York is west of me.

4 I am the fourth-smallest state. The Pacific Ocean borders me on all sides.

5 I am the fifth-smallest state. Delaware is south of me.

6 I am the sixth-smallest state. Vermont and New Hampshire are north of me.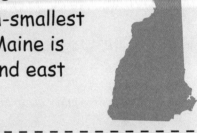

7 I am the seventh-smallest state. Maine is north and east of me.

8 I am the eighth-smallest state. New York is west of me.

9 I am the ninth-smallest state. Delaware is east of me.

10 I am the tenth-smallest state. Virginia is south and east of me.

Massachusetts

The United States
Set 2

©2005 by Evan-Moor Corp. • EMC 3717

Rhode Island

The United States
Set 2

©2005 by Evan-Moor Corp. • EMC 3717

New Hampshire

The United States
Set 2

©2005 by Evan-Moor Corp. • EMC 3717

Delaware

The United States
Set 2

©2005 by Evan-Moor Corp. • EMC 3717

Vermont

The United States
Set 2

©2005 by Evan-Moor Corp. • EMC 3717

Connecticut

The United States
Set 2

©2005 by Evan-Moor Corp. • EMC 3717

Maryland

The United States
Set 2

©2005 by Evan-Moor Corp. • EMC 3717

Hawaii

The United States
Set 2

©2005 by Evan-Moor Corp. • EMC 3717

West Virginia

The United States
Set 2

©2005 by Evan-Moor Corp. • EMC 3717

New Jersey

The United States
Set 2

©2005 by Evan-Moor Corp. • EMC 3717

The United States

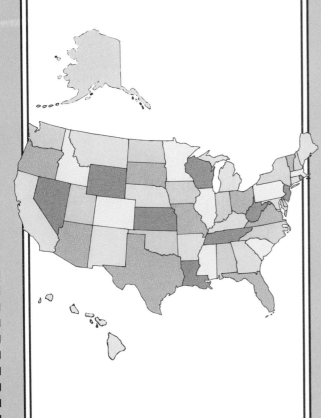

Lift the flap to check
your answers.

The United States

Set 1

You should have colored these states on the map:

Alaska
Arizona
California
Colorado
Montana
Nevada
New Mexico
Oregon
Texas
Wyoming

Western part of the U.S.

Set 2

You should have colored these ten states on the map:

Connecticut
Delaware
Hawaii
Maryland
Massachusetts
New Hampshire
New Jersey
Rhode Island
Vermont
West Virginia

Eastern part of the U.S.

The United States

©2005 by Evan-Moor Corp. • EMC 3717

The United States

©2005 by Evan-Moor Corp. • EMC 3717

Parts of a Map

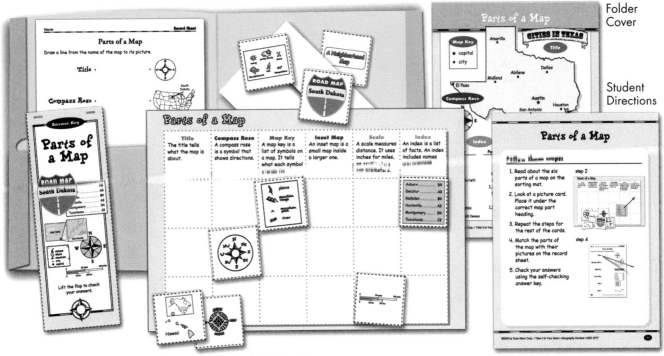

Folder Cover

Student Directions

Picture Cards and Sorting Mat

Preparing the Center

1. Prepare a folder following the directions on page 3.

    Cover—page 91

    Student Directions—page 93

    Sorting Mat—pages 95 and 97

    Picture Cards—pages 99 and 101

    Self-Checking Key—page 103

2. Reproduce a supply of the record sheet on page 90. Place copies in the left-hand pocket of the folder.

Using the Center

1. The student reads each heading on the sorting mat to learn about the six parts of a map.

2. Next, the student places each picture card under the matching heading on the sorting mat. The picture cards are self-checking.

3. Then the student matches the name of each of the six parts of a map with its picture on the record sheet.

4. Finally, the student uses the self-checking key to check answers.

Parts of a Map

Draw a line from the name of the map part to its picture.

Title •

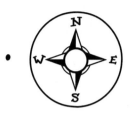

Compass Rose •

Map Key •

Inset Map •

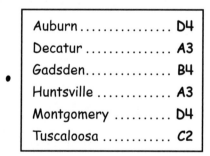

Scale •

Index •

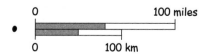

Parts of a Map

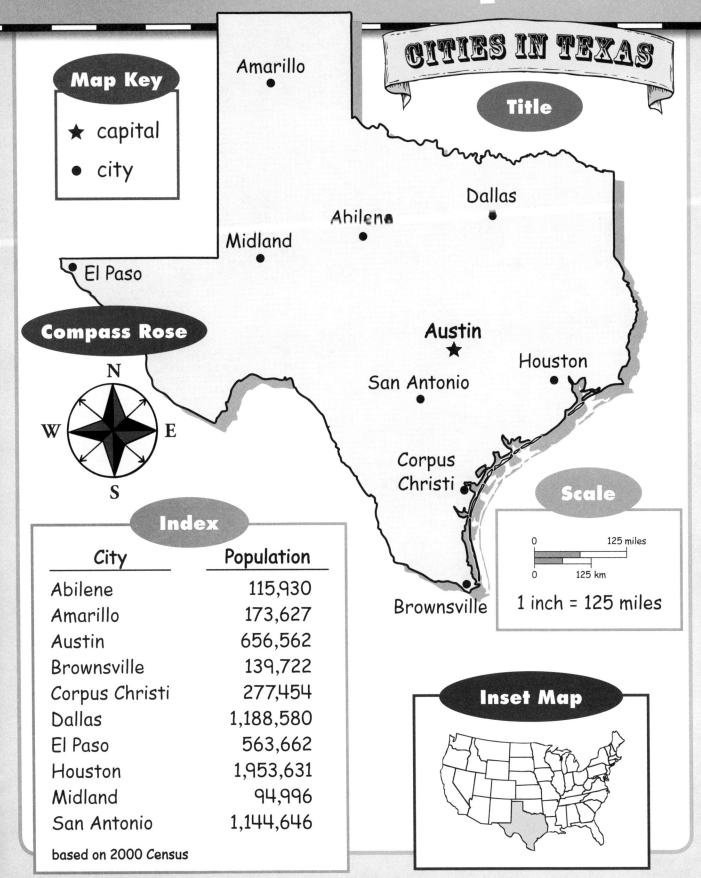

Map Key

★ capital
● city

CITIES IN TEXAS

Title

Amarillo
•

Dallas
•

Abilene
•

Midland
•

El Paso
•

Compass Rose

N
W   E
S

Austin
★

Houston
•

San Antonio
•

Corpus
Christi
•

Scale

0   125 miles

0   125 km

1 inch = 125 miles

Brownsville
•

Index

City	Population
Abilene	115,930
Amarillo	173,627
Austin	656,562
Brownsville	139,722
Corpus Christi	277,454
Dallas	1,188,580
El Paso	563,662
Houston	1,953,631
Midland	94,996
San Antonio	1,144,646

based on 2000 Census

Inset Map

Parts of a Map

Follow these steps:

1. Read about the six parts of a map on the sorting mat.

2. Look at a picture card. Place it under the correct map part heading.

3. Repeat the steps for the rest of the cards.

4. Match the parts of the map with their pictures on the record sheet.

5. Check your answers using the self-checking answer key.

step 2

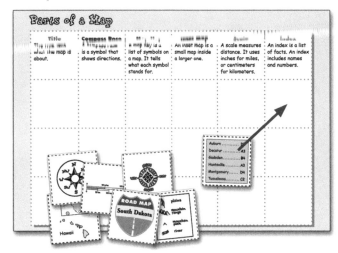

step 4

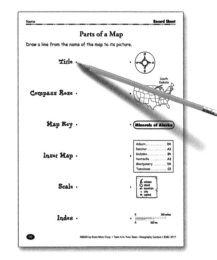

Parts of a Map

Title	**Compass Rose**	**Map Key**
The title tells what the map is about.	A compass rose is a symbol that shows directions.	A map key is a list of symbols on a map. It tells what each symbol stands for.

Inset Map

An inset map is a small map inside a larger one.

Scale

A scale measures distance. It uses inches for miles, or centimeters for kilometers.

Index

An index is a list of facts. An index includes names and numbers.

glue

ROAD MAP

South Dakota

A World Map

A Neighborhood Map

N
W   E
S

N
NW   NE
W   E
SW   SE
S

NORTH
WEST   EAST
SOUTH

sunny   partly cloudy   snow

thunderstorms   rain   50°   temperature

plains

mountain range

mountain peak

river

state border

international border

national capital

Title

Parts of a Map

Title

Parts of a Map

Title

Parts of a Map

Compass Rose

Parts of a Map

Compass Rose

Parts of a Map

Compass Rose

Parts of a Map

Key

Parts of a Map

Key

Parts of a Map

Key

Parts of a Map

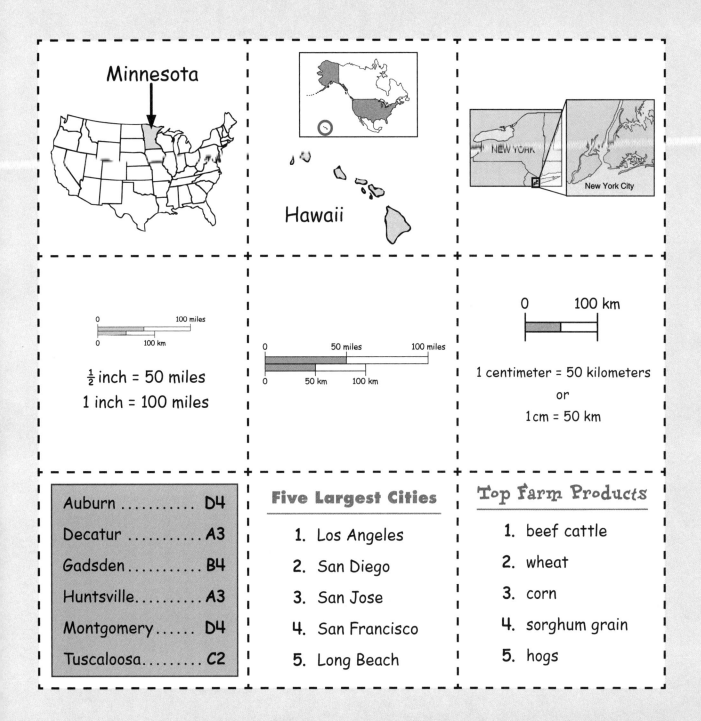

Minnesota

Hawaii

NEW YORK

New York City

0   100 miles
0   100 km

½ inch = 50 miles
1 inch = 100 miles

0   50 miles   100 miles
0   50 km   100 km

0   100 km

1 centimeter = 50 kilometers
or
1cm = 50 km

Auburn	D4
Decatur	A3
Gadsden	B4
Huntsville..........	A3
Montgomery......	D4
Tuscaloosa.........	C2

Five Largest Cities

1. Los Angeles
2. San Diego
3. San Jose
4. San Francisco
5. Long Beach

Top Farm Products

1. beef cattle
2. wheat
3. corn
4. sorghum grain
5. hogs

Inset Map

Parts of a Map
©2005 by Evan-Moor Corp. • EMC 3717

Inset Map

Parts of a Map
©2005 by Evan-Moor Corp. • EMC 3717

Inset Map

Parts of a Map
©2005 by Evan-Moor Corp. • EMC 3717

Scale

Parts of a Map
©2005 by Evan-Moor Corp. • EMC 3717

Scale

Parts of a Map
©2005 by Evan-Moor Corp. • EMC 3717

Scale

Parts of a Map
©2005 by Evan-Moor Corp. • EMC 3717

Index

Parts of a Map
©2005 by Evan-Moor Corp. • EMC 3717

Index

Parts of a Map
©2005 by Evan-Moor Corp. • EMC 3717

Index

Parts of a Map
©2005 by Evan-Moor Corp. • EMC 3717

Parts of a Map

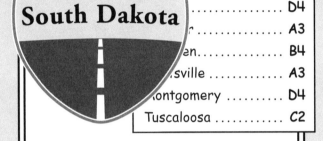

ROAD MAP
South Dakota

.... D4
.... A3
en.............. B4
sville A3
Montgomery D4
Tuscaloosa C2

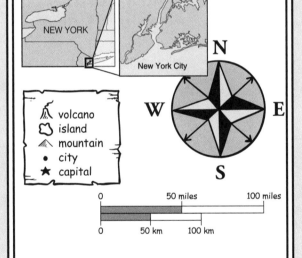

NEW YORK

New York City

N
W   E
S

🌋 volcano
🏝 island
⛰ mountain
• city
★ capital

0   50 miles   100 miles
0   50 km   100 km

Lift the flap to check
your answers.

Parts of a Map

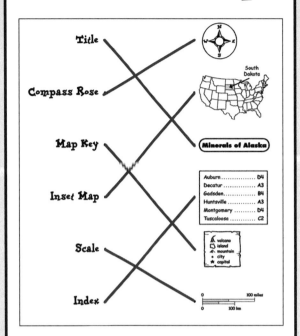

Title

Compass Rose

Map Key

Inset Map

Scale

Index

South Dakota

Minerals of Alaska

Auburn	D4
Decatur	A3
Gadsden	B4
Huntsville	A3
Montgomery	D4
Tuscaloosa	C2

🌋 volcano
🏝 island
⛰ mountain
• city
★ capital

0   100 miles
0   100 km

Parts of a Map

Parts of a Map

Reading a Road Map

Folder Cover

Student Directions

Question Cards and Road Maps

Preparing the Center

1. Prepare a folder following the directions on page 3.

   Cover—page 107

   Student Directions—page 109

   Question Cards—pages 113 and 115
   • Set 1—purple
   • Set 2—green

   Self-Checking Key—page 117

2. Laminate the road maps on pages 111 and 112. Place the two-sided map card in the right-hand pocket of the folder for the student to use with the question cards.

3. Reproduce a supply of the record sheet on page 106. Place copies in the left-hand pocket of the folder.

Using the Center

1. The student takes a set of question cards, the matching road map, and a record sheet. The student circles the set number on the record sheet.

2. The student studies the map that matches the set of question cards.

3. Next, the student reads a question card. The student looks at the map to find the answer.

4. Then the student records the answer on the record sheet.

5. The student repeats the steps for the remaining cards.

6. Finally, the student uses the self-checking key to check answers.

Circle: Set 1   Set 2

Reading a Road Map

Write the answers to the question cards.
Write the letter **A** or the letter **B**.

1. _____

2. _____

3. _____

4. _____

5. _____

6. _____

7. _____

8. _____

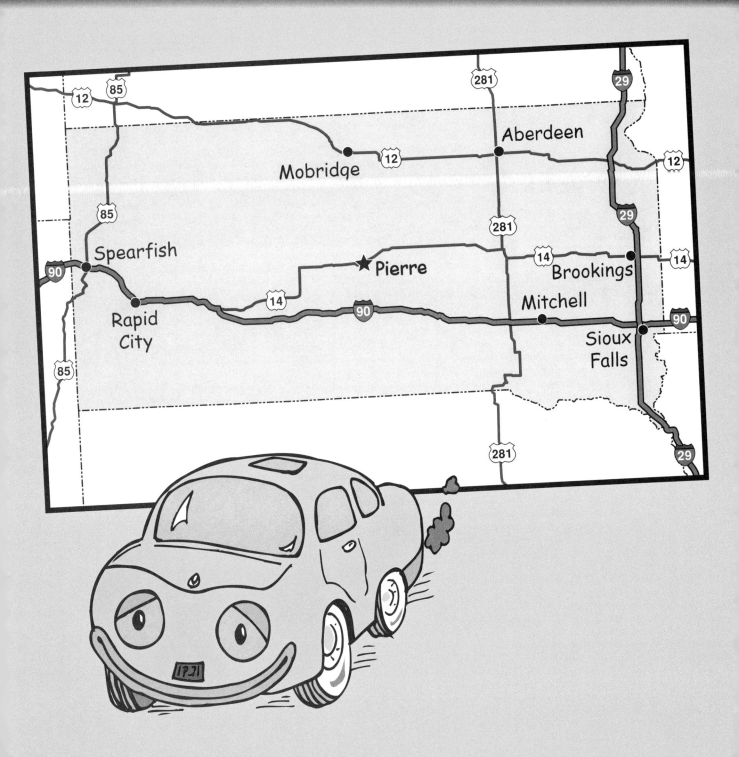

Reading a Road Map

Follow these steps:

1. Take a set of question cards, the road map, and a record sheet. Circle the set number on the record sheet.

2. Turn the road map to the correct side. Read and study the map.

3. Next, read a question card. Choose which answer, A or B, is correct.

4. Then write the letter choice on the record sheet.

5. Repeat the steps for the rest of the cards.

6. Check your answers using the self-checking answer key.

step 2

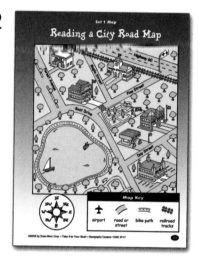

step 3

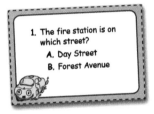

step 4

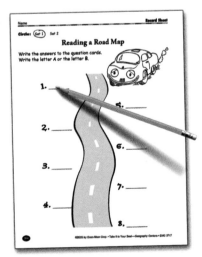

Reading a City Road Map

Map Key

| airport | road or street | bike path | railroad tracks |

Reading a State Road Map

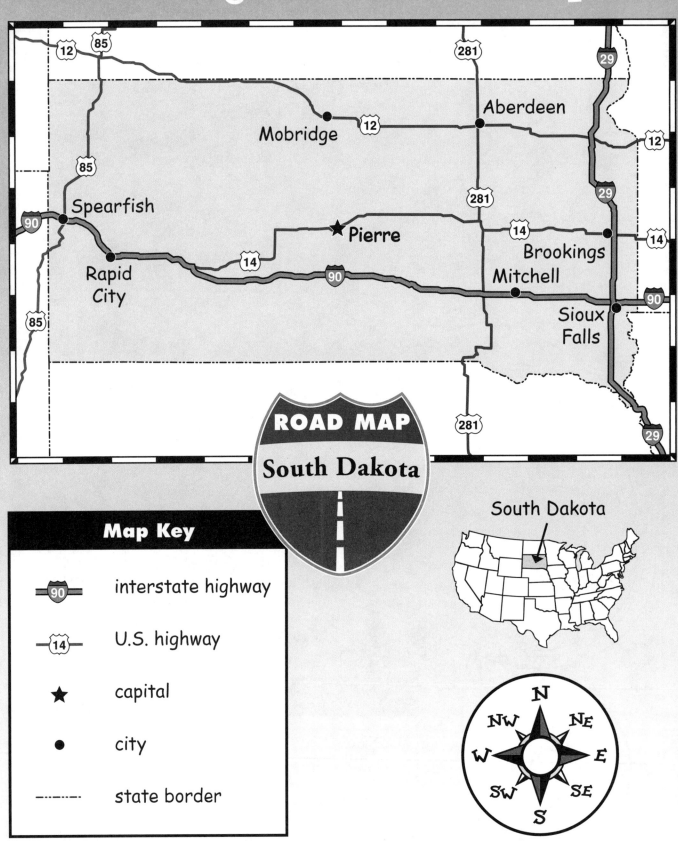

ROAD MAP
South Dakota

Map Key

🛡️ 90   interstate highway

🛡️ 14   U.S. highway

★   capital

●   city

---·---   state border

South Dakota

1. The fire station is on which street?

   A. Day Street

   B. Forest Avenue

2. You enter the school from which street?

   A. Maple Street

   B. Pine Street

3. Which road leads to the airport?

   A. Highway 60

   B. Pine Street

4. Which one is closer to the park?

   A. mall

   B. school

5. What do you cross to get to Highway 60?

   A. bike path

   B. railroad tracks

6. The bike path and lake are near which street?

   A. Boat Drive

   B. Maple Street

7. The train station is on which road?

   A. Highway 60

   B. Maple Street

8. The police station is on which street?

   A. Forest Avenue

   B. Boat Drive

Reading a Road Map
Set 1

Reading a Road Map
Set 1

Reading a Road Map
Set 1

Reading a Road Map
Set 1

Reading a Road Map
Set 1

Reading a Road Map
Set 1

Reading a Road Map
Set 1

Reading a Road Map
Set 1

1. What does the road map show?

   A. major highways in South Dakota

   B. streets and highways in South Dakota

5. Which city is farther west on Interstate 90?

   A. Sioux Falls

   B. Spearfish

2. Which interstate highway runs north and south?

   A. Interstate 29

   B. Interstate 90

6. Where is Sioux Falls?

   A. at the intersection of Interstate Highways 29 and 90

   B. between Brookings and Mitchell

3. The capital of South Dakota is on which highway?

   A. U.S. Highway 281

   B. U.S. Highway 14

7. Which interstate highway is longer?

   A. Interstate 29

   B. Interstate 90

4. Which two cities are on U.S. Highway 12?

   A. Aberdeen and Mobridge

   B. Brookings and Rapid City

8. How do you travel from Brookings to Pierre?

   A. east on U.S. Highway 14

   B. west on U.S. Highway 14

Reading a Road Map
Set 2

©2005 by Evan-Moor Corp. • EMC 3717

Reading a Road Map
Set 2

©2005 by Evan-Moor Corp. • EMC 3717

Reading a Road Map
Set 2

©2005 by Evan-Moor Corp. • EMC 3717

Reading a Road Map
Set 2

©2005 by Evan-Moor Corp. • EMC 3717

Reading a Road Map
Set 2

©2005 by Evan-Moor Corp. • EMC 3717

Reading a Road Map
Set 2

©2005 by Evan-Moor Corp. • EMC 3717

Reading a Road Map
Set 2

©2005 by Evan-Moor Corp. • EMC 3717

Reading a Road Map
Set 2

©2005 by Evan-Moor Corp. • EMC 3717

Reading a Road Map

◀ Sioux Falls 125 miles
Pierre 100 miles ▶

Lift the flap to check your answers.

Reading a Road Map

Set 1

1. A
2. B
3. A
4. B
5. B
6. A
7. B
8. A

Set 2

1. A
2. A
3. B
4. A
5. B
6. A
7. B
8. B

Reading a Road Map

©2005 by Evan-Moor Corp. • EMC 3717

Reading a Road Map

©2005 by Evan-Moor Corp. • EMC 3717

Landforms

Puzzle Pieces and Landform Picture Map

Preparing the Center

1. Prepare a folder following the directions on page 3.

   Cover—page 121

   Student Directions—page 123

   Puzzle Pieces—pages 127–133
   - Terms and Definitions
   - Pictures

   Self-Checking Key—page 135

2. Laminate the landform picture map on page 125. Place the map card in the right-hand pocket of the folder for the student to use as a reference.

3. Reproduce a supply of the record sheet on page 120. Place copies in the left-hand pocket of the folder.

Using the Center

1. The student studies the landform picture map.

2. Next, the student matches the term and picture pieces to complete a puzzle. The puzzles are self-checking.

3. The student repeats the steps to complete the rest of the puzzles.

4. On the record sheet, the student labels the landform picture map.

5. Finally, the student uses the self-checking key to check answers.

Landforms

Write the name of the landform that matches the number on the map. Use the words in the box to help you.

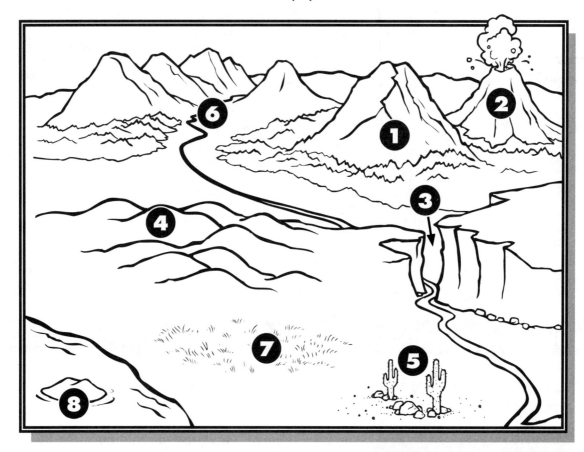

1. _____

2. _____

3. _____

4. _____

5. _____

6. _____

7. _____

8. _____

Word Box

canyon	mountain
desert	plain
hill	valley
island	volcano

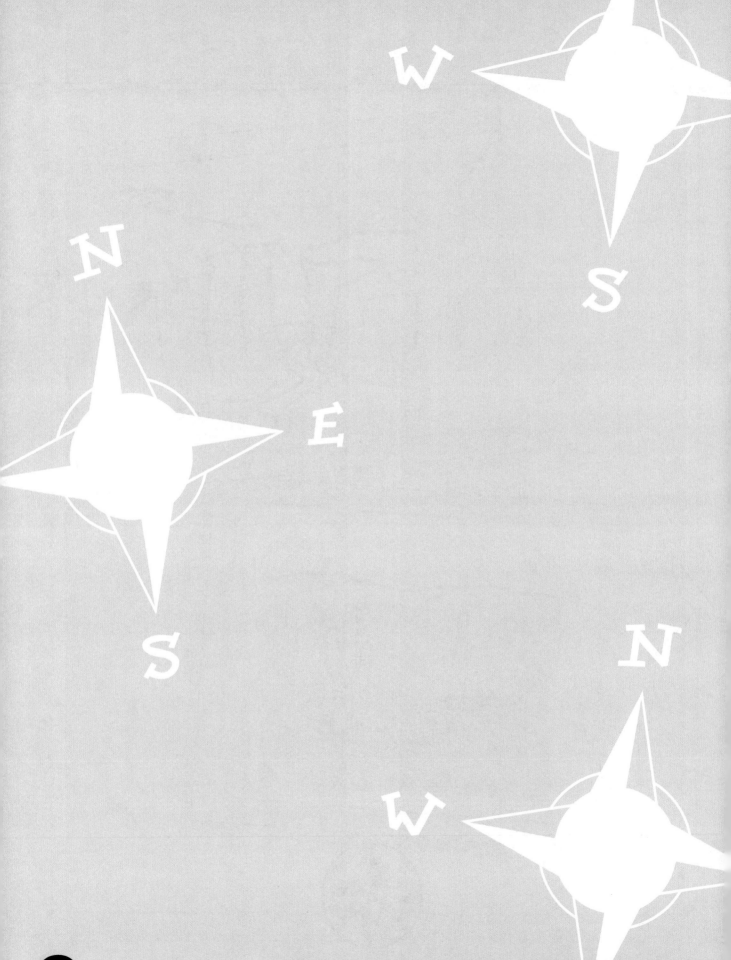

Landforms

Follow these steps:

1. Match the name and definition of one landform with its picture to make a puzzle.

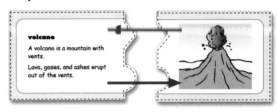

step 1

2. Repeat step 1 to make the rest of the puzzles.

3. On the record sheet, write the names of the landforms that are on the map.

step 3

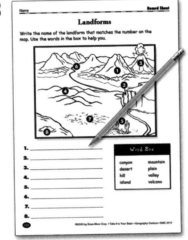

4. Check your answers using the self-checking answer key.

step 4

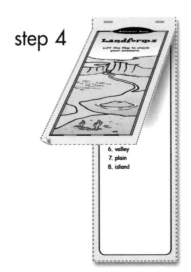

Landforms

The land on Earth is not all flat. The land takes many shapes. The different shapes are called **landforms**. This picture map shows eight of Earth's landforms.

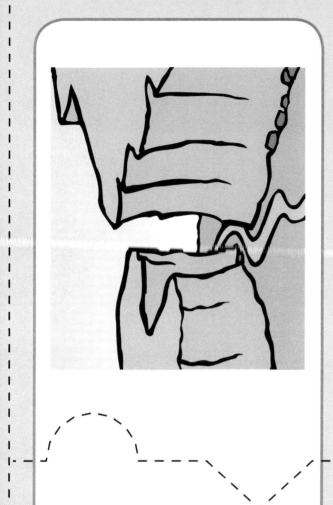

canyon

A canyon is a deep valley with steep sides.

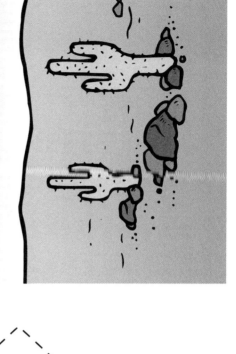

desert

A desert is a dry area. It is often sandy or rocky.

A desert is very hot in the daytime.

Landforms

Landforms

Landforms

Landforms

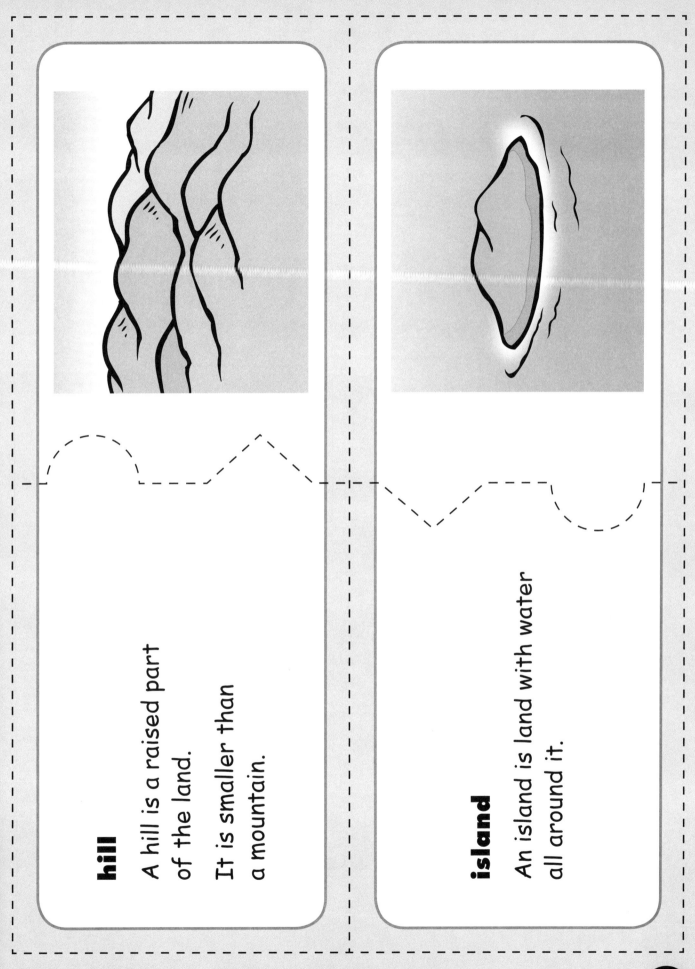

hill

A hill is a raised part of the land.

It is smaller than a mountain.

island

An island is land with water all around it.

©2005 by Evan-Moor Corp. • EMC 3717

Landforms

©2005 by Evan-Moor Corp. • EMC 3717

Landforms

©2005 by Evan-Moor Corp. • EMC 3717

Landforms

©2005 by Evan-Moor Corp. • EMC 3717

Landforms

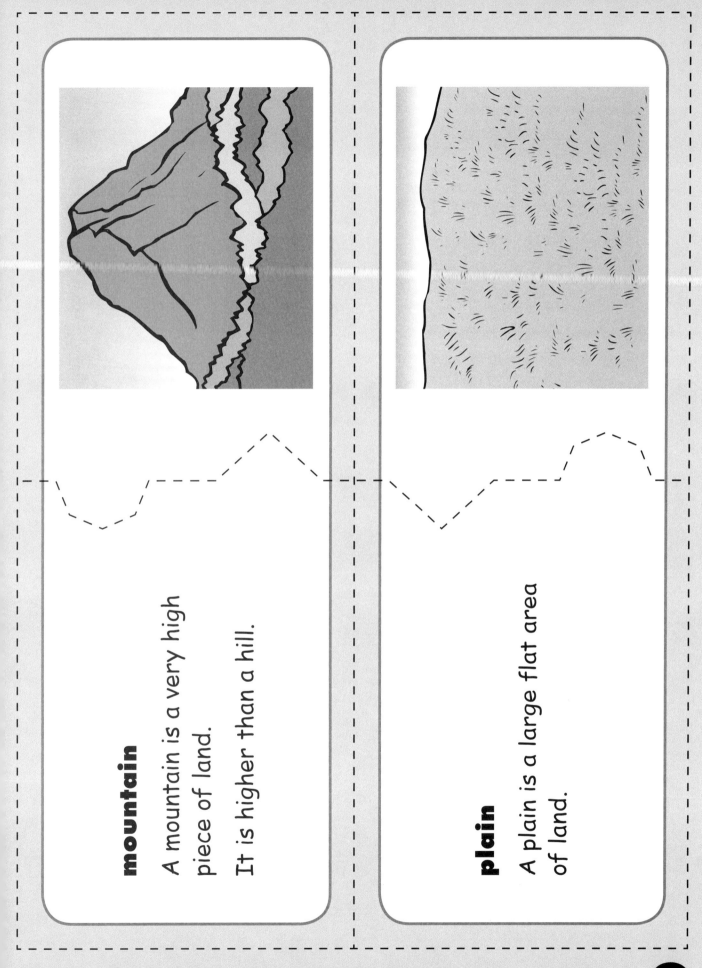

mountain

A mountain is a very high piece of land.

It is higher than a hill.

plain

A plain is a large flat area of land.

Landforms

Landforms

Landforms

Landforms

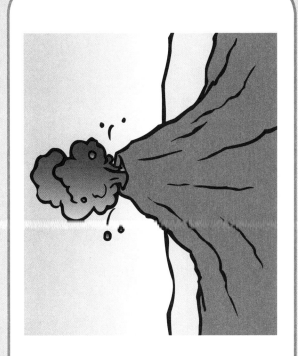

valley

A valley is an area of low ground between two hills or between two mountains.

volcano

A volcano is a mountain with vents.

Lava, gases, and ashes erupt out of the vents.

Landforms

Landforms

Landforms

Landforms

Landforms

Lift the flap to check your answers.

Landforms

1. mountain
2. volcano
3. canyon
4. hill
5. desert
6. valley
7. plain
8. island

Landforms

Landforms

Florida's Waterways

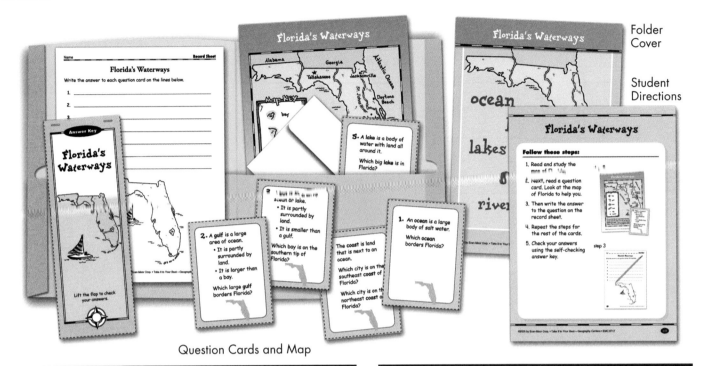

Folder Cover

Student Directions

Question Cards and Map

Preparing the Center

1. Prepare a folder following the directions on page 3.

    Cover—page 139

    Student Directions—page 141

    Question Cards—pages 145 and 147

    Self-Checking Answer Key—
    page 149

2. Laminate the map of Florida on page 143. Place the map card in the right-hand pocket of the folder for the student to use with the question cards.

3. Reproduce a supply of the record sheet on page 138. Place copies in the left-hand pocket of the folder.

Using the Center

1. The student studies the map of Florida.

2. Next, the student reads a question card. The student uses the map of Florida to help answer the question.

3. Then the student records the answer on the record sheet.

4. The student repeats the steps for the remaining question cards.

5. Finally, the student uses the self-checking key to check answers.

Florida's Waterways

Write the answer to each question card on the lines below.

1. _____

2. _____

3. _____

4. _____

5. _____

6. _____

7. _____

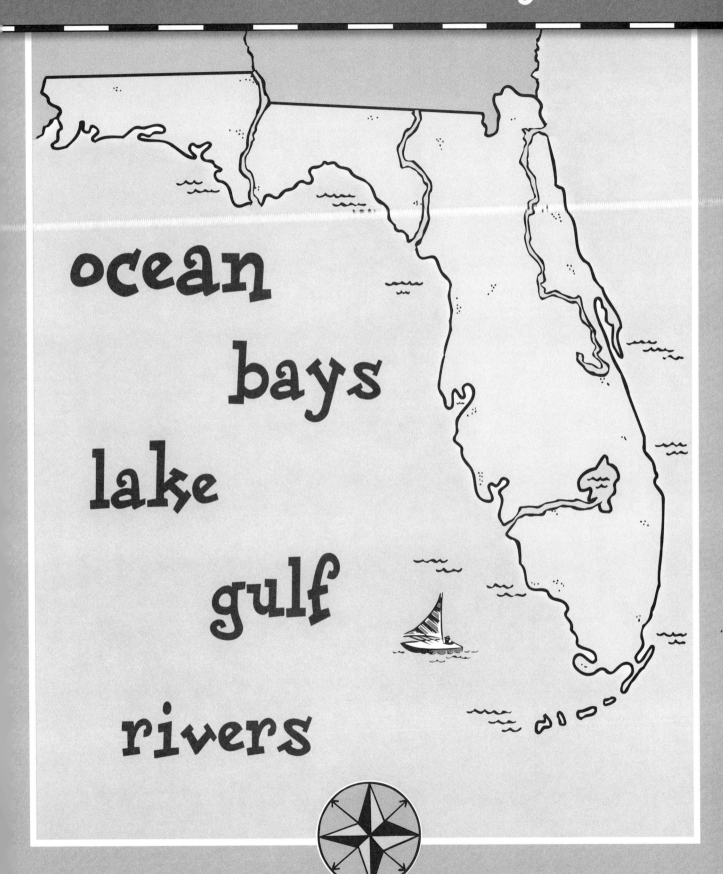

ocean

bays

lake

gulf

rivers

Florida's Waterways

Follow these steps:

1. Read and study the map of Florida.

2. Next, read a question card. Look at the map of Florida to help you.

3. Then write the answer to the question on the record sheet.

4. Repeat the steps for the rest of the cards.

5. Check your answers using the self-checking answer key.

step 2

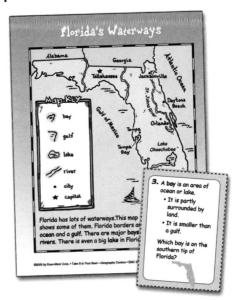

step 3

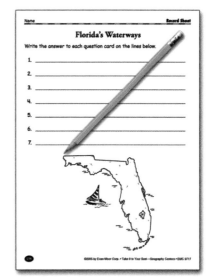

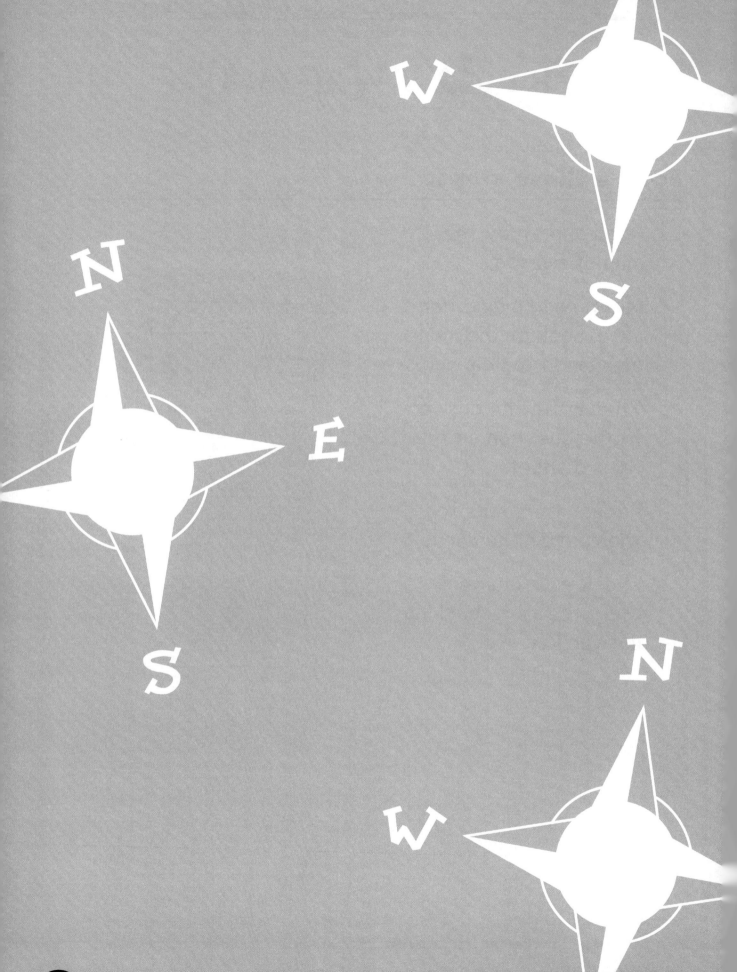

Florida's Waterways

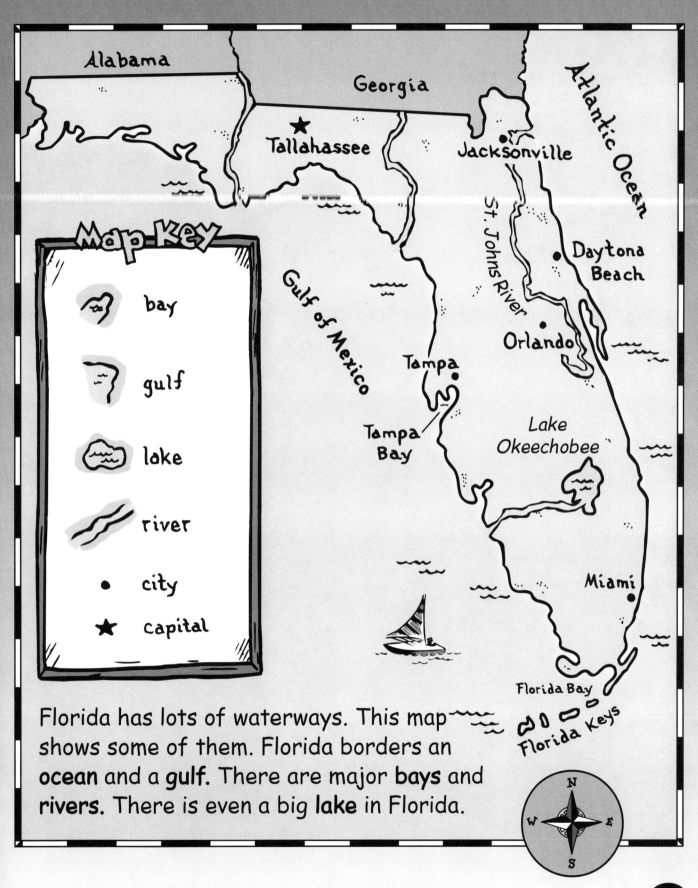

Map Key

- bay
- gulf
- lake
- river
- • city
- ★ capital

Alabama

Georgia

★ Tallahassee

Jacksonville

Atlantic Ocean

St. Johns River

Gulf of Mexico

• Daytona Beach

Orlando

Tampa

Tampa Bay

Lake Okeechobee

Miami

Florida Bay

Florida Keys

Florida has lots of waterways. This map shows some of them. Florida borders an **ocean** and a **gulf**. There are major **bays** and **rivers**. There is even a big **lake** in Florida.

1. An **ocean** is a large body of salt water.

Which **ocean** borders Florida?

2. A **gulf** is a large area of ocean.

- It is partly surrounded by land.
- It is larger than a bay.

Which large **gulf** borders Florida?

3. A **bay** is an area of ocean or lake.

- It is partly surrounded by land.
- It is smaller than a gulf.

Which **bay** is on the southern tip of Florida?

4. A **river** is a large stream of water that flows across land.

Which **river** is labeled on the map of Florida?

Florida's Waterways
©2005 by Evan-Moor Corp. • EMC 3717

Florida's Waterways
©2005 by Evan-Moor Corp. • EMC 3717

Florida's Waterways
©2005 by Evan-Moor Corp. • EMC 3717

Florida's Waterways
©2005 by Evan-Moor Corp. • EMC 3717

5. A **lake** is a body of water with land all around it.

Which big **lake** is in Florida?

What kind of waterway flows from the lake?

7. On a map, a **city** in a state is shown with a dot.

Which **city** is in western Florida?

Which waterway is named after it?

6. On a map, the **capital** of a state is shown with a star.

What is the **capital** of Florida?

What kind of waterway is both east and west of it?

8. The **coast** is land that is next to an ocean.

Which city is on the southeast **coast** of Florida?

Which city is on the northeast **coast** of Florida?

Florida's Waterways
2005 by Evan-Moor Corp. • EMC 3717

Florida's Waterways
2005 by Evan-Moor Corp. • EMC 3717

Florida's Waterways

Lift the flap to check
your answers.

Florida's Waterways

1. Atlantic Ocean
2. Gulf of Mexico
3. Florida Bay
4. St. Johns River
5. Lake Okeechobee; river
6. Tallahassee; river
7. Tampa; Tampa Bay
8. Miami; Daytona Beach

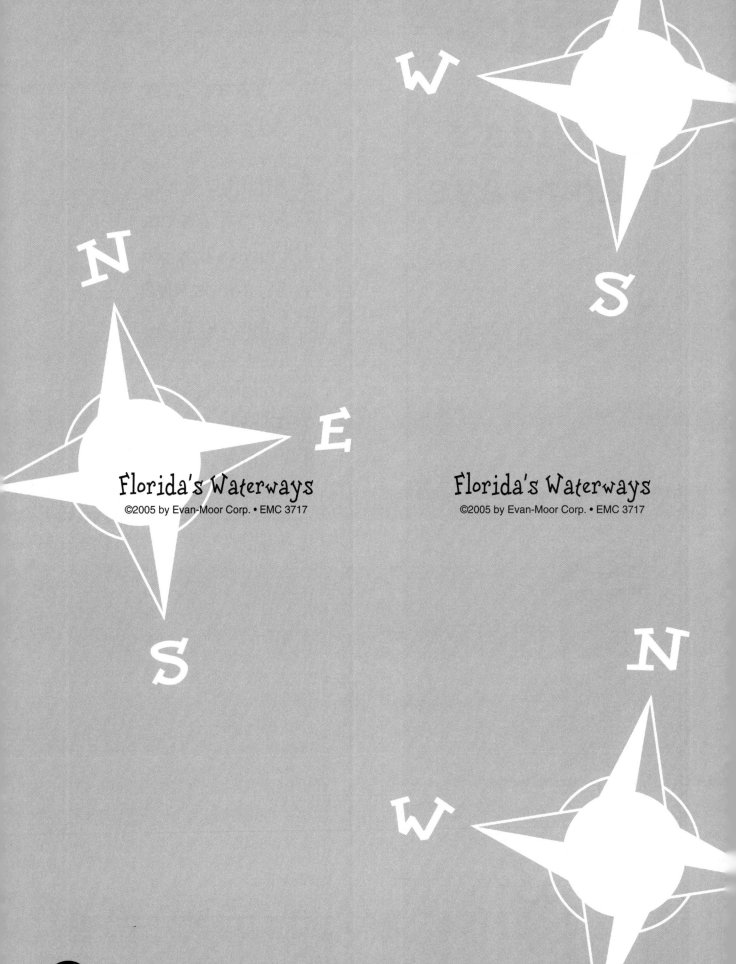

Florida's Waterways

©2005 by Evan-Moor Corp. • EMC 3717

Florida's Waterways

©2005 by Evan-Moor Corp. • EMC 3717

A Trip to California

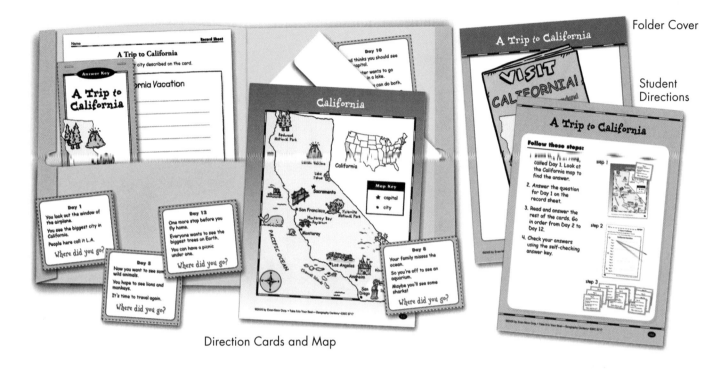

Folder Cover

Student
Directions

Direction Cards and Map

Preparing the Center

1. Prepare a folder following the directions on page 3.

    Cover—page 153

    Student Directions—page 155

    Direction Cards—pages 159 and 161

    Self-Checking Key—page 163

2. Laminate the tourist map of California on page 157. Place the map in the right-hand pocket of the folder for the student to use with the direction cards.

3. Reproduce a supply of the record sheet on page 152. Place copies in the left-hand pocket of the folder.

Using the Center

1. The student begins with Day 1 of the trip. The student reads the direction card and uses the map of California to help answer the question.

2. On the record sheet, the student records the name of the tourist attraction described on the Day 1 card.

3. The student continues the same process in chronological order—from Day 2 to Day 12.

4. Finally, the student uses the self-checking key to check answers.

A Trip to California

Write the name of the place or city described on the card.

California Vacation

Day 1 _____

Day 2 _____

Day 3 _____

Day 4 _____

Day 5 _____

Day 6 _____

Day 7 _____

Day 8 _____

Day 9 _____

Day 10 _____

Day 11 _____

Day 12 _____

A Trip to California

HOLLYWOOD

ROAR!

Lift the flap to check
your answers.

A Trip to California

1. Los Angeles
2. Hollywood
3. Disneyland
4. Pacific Ocean;
   Channel Islands
5. San Diego Zoo
6. Mojave Desert
7. Yosemite National
   Park
8. Monterey Bay
   Aquarium
9. San Francisco
10. Sacramento; Lake
    Tahoe
11. Lassen Volcano
12. Redwood National
    Park

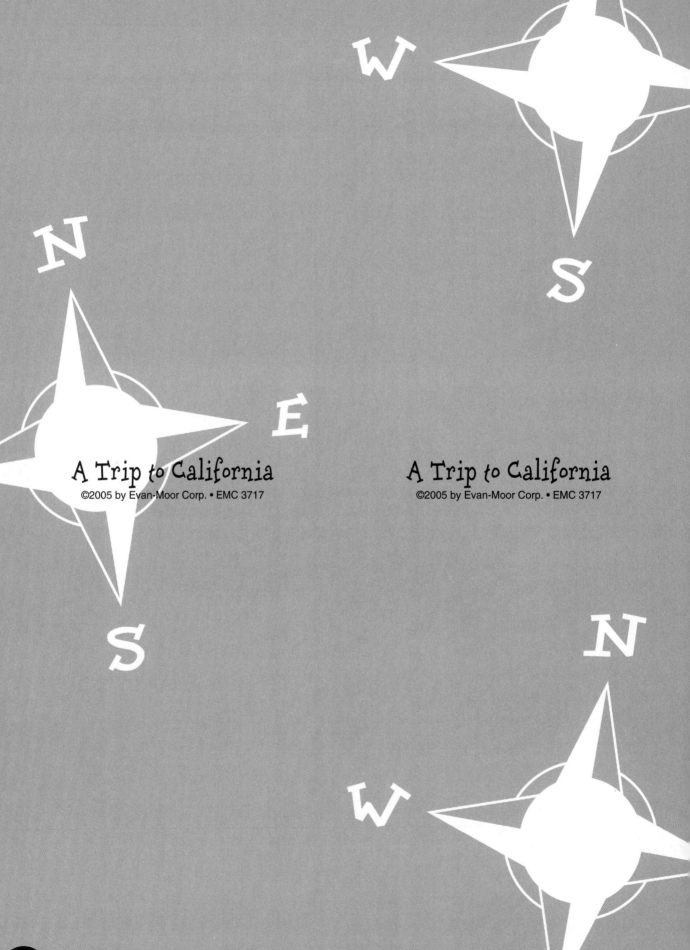

A Trip to California

©2005 by Evan-Moor Corp. • EMC 3717

A Trip to California

©2005 by Evan-Moor Corp. • EMC 3717

Famous Monuments

Folder Cover

Student Directions

Task Cards

Preparing the Center

1. Prepare a folder following the directions on page 3.

    Cover—page 167

    Student Directions—page 169

    Task Cards—pages 171–175
    • Picture Cards
    • Information Cards

    Self-Checking Key—page 177

2. Reproduce a supply of the record sheet on page 166. Place copies in the left-hand pocket of the folder.

Using the Center

1. The student reads an information card about a famous monument.

2. Next, the student finds the matching picture card. The cards are self-checking.

3. Then the student writes the name of the famous monument on the record sheet.

4. The student repeats the steps for the remaining cards.

5. On the record sheet, the student also writes the city where all three monument pictures are found.

6. Finally, the student uses the self-checking key to check answers.

Famous Monuments

Part 1

Write the name of each monument on the correct line.

1. _____

2. _____

3. _____

4. _____

5. _____

6. _____

7. _____

8. _____

Part 2

The White House

The Washington Monument

The U.S. Capitol

These three famous monuments are all found in the city of

_____ .

Famous Monuments

Follow these steps:

1. Read an information card about a famous monument.

2. Next, find the picture of the monument that matches the information.

3. Then write the name of the monument on the record sheet.

4. Repeat the steps to match the rest of the cards.

5. Finish the record sheet. Write the city where three famous monuments are found.

6. Check your answers using the self-checking answer key.

step 1

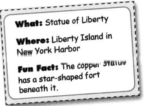

What: Statue of Liberty

Where: Liberty Island in New York Harbor

Fun Fact: The copper statue has a star-shaped fort beneath it.

step 2

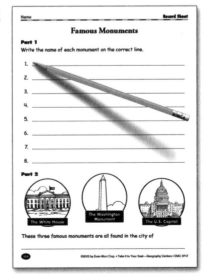

step 3

Famous Monuments

©2005 by Evan-Moor Corp. • EMC 3717

Famous Monuments

©2005 by Evan-Moor Corp. • EMC 3717

Famous Monuments

©2005 by Evan-Moor Corp. • EMC 3717

Famous Monuments

©2005 by Evan-Moor Corp. • EMC 3717

Famous Monuments

©2005 by Evan-Moor Corp. • EMC 3717

Famous Monuments

©2005 by Evan-Moor Corp. • EMC 3717

Famous Monuments

©2005 by Evan-Moor Corp. • EMC 3717

Famous Monuments

©2005 by Evan-Moor Corp. • EMC 3717

What: Statue of Liberty

Where: Liberty Island in New York Harbor

Fun Fact: The copper statue has a star-shaped fort beneath it.

What: Mount Rushmore

Where: South Dakota

Fun Fact: The head of George Washington is as tall as a five-story building.

What: Washington Monument

Where: Washington, D.C.

Fun Fact: There are 898 steps to the top of the monument.

What: Gateway Arch

Where: St. Louis, Missouri

Fun Fact: The arch is 630 feet tall and is made of steel.

What: White House

Where: Washington, D.C.

Fun Fact: Every president except George Washington has lived there.

What: Golden Gate Bridge

Where: San Francisco, California

Fun Fact: The suspension bridge is not really golden. It is painted orange.

What: Space Needle

Where: Seattle, Washington

Fun Fact: The top looks like a flying saucer.

What: U.S. Capitol

Where: Washington, D.C.

Fun Fact: Government leaders work in the 540 rooms of the U.S. Capitol.

Famous Monuments

©2005 by Evan-Moor Corp. • EMC 3717

Famous Monuments

©2005 by Evan-Moor Corp. • EMC 3717

Famous Monuments

©2005 by Evan-Moor Corp. • EMC 3717

Famous Monuments

©2005 by Evan-Moor Corp. • EMC 3717

Famous Monuments

©2005 by Evan-Moor Corp. • EMC 3717

Famous Monuments

©2005 by Evan-Moor Corp. • EMC 3717

Famous Monuments

©2005 by Evan-Moor Corp. • EMC 3717

Famous Monuments

©2005 by Evan-Moor Corp. • EMC 3717

Famous Monuments

Lift the flap to check your answers.

Famous Monuments

Part 1

1. Statue of Liberty
2. Washington Monument
3. White House
4. Space Needle
5. Mount Rushmore
6. Gateway Arch
7. Golden Gate Bridge
8. U.S. Capitol

Part 2

The White House, the Washington Monument, and the U.S. Capitol are all located in **Washington, D.C.**

Famous Monuments

©2005 by Evan-Moor Corp. • EMC 3717

Famous Monuments

©2005 by Evan-Moor Corp. • EMC 3717

North America

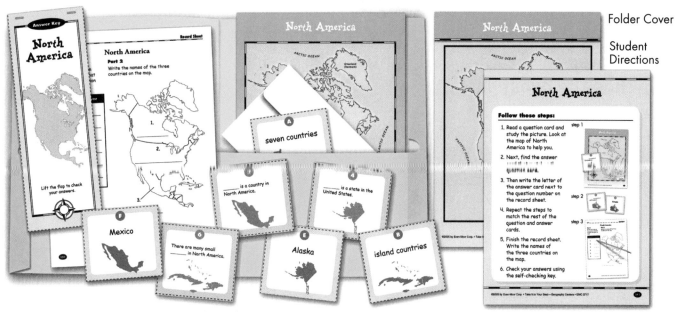

Task Cards and Map

Preparing the Center

1. Prepare a folder following the directions on page 3.

   Cover—page 181

   Student Directions—page 183

   Task Cards—pages 187 and 189
   • Question Cards—green
   • Answer Cards—blue

   Self-Checking Key—page 191

2. Laminate the map of North America on page 185. Place the map card in the right-hand pocket of the folder for the student to use with the task cards.

3. Reproduce a supply of the record sheet on page 180. Place copies in the left-hand pocket of the folder.

Using the Center

1. The student reads a question card. The student uses the map of North America to help answer the question.

2. Next, the student matches the question card with the correct answer card. The cards are self-checking.

3. Then the student writes the letter of the answer card next to the question number on the record sheet.

4. The student repeats the steps for the remaining cards.

5. The student also labels three countries on the North America map on the record sheet.

6. Finally, the student uses the self-checking key to check answers.

North America

Part 1

Write the letter on the answer card that matches the question card.

Question	Answer
1.	_____
2.	_____
3.	_____
4.	_____
5.	_____
6.	_____

Part 2

Write the names of the three countries on the map.

1 _____

2 _____

3 _____

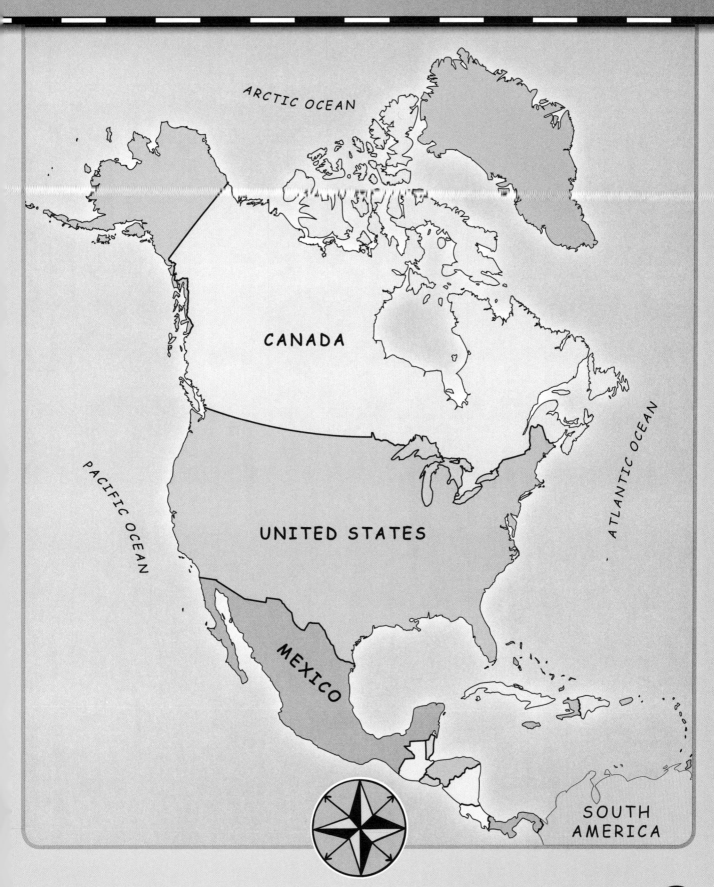

ARCTIC OCEAN

CANADA

PACIFIC OCEAN

UNITED STATES

ATLANTIC OCEAN

MEXICO

SOUTH
AMERICA

North America

Follow these steps:

1. Read a question card and study the picture. Look at the map of North America to help you.

2. Next, find the answer card that matches the question card.

3. Then write the letter of the answer card next to the question number on the record sheet.

4. Repeat the steps to match the rest of the question and answer cards.

5. Finish the record sheet. Write the names of the three countries on the map.

6. Check your answers using the self-checking key.

step 1

step 2

step 3

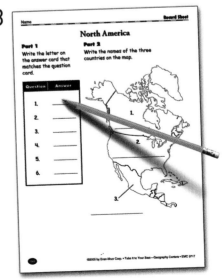

North America

ARCTIC OCEAN

Greenland
(Denmark)

Alaska
(USA)

CANADA

PACIFIC OCEAN

ATLANTIC OCEAN

UNITED STATES

MEXICO

THE BAHAMAS

CUBA

DOMINICAN REPUBLIC

JAMAICA

HAITI

Puerto Rico
(USA)

BELIZE

HONDURAS

NICARAGUA

GUATEMALA

COSTA RICA

EL SALVADOR

SOUTH AMERICA

PANAMA

N
W   E
S

1

_____ is a country in North America.

2

_____ is a country in North America.

3

_____ is a country in North America.

4

_____ is a state in the United States.

5

These _____ are part of North America.

6

There are many small _____ in North America.

North America

North America

North America

North America

North America

North America

A seven countries

B island countries

C The United States

D Canada

E Alaska

F Mexico

North America

©2005 by Evan-Moor Corp. • EMC 3717

North America

©2005 by Evan-Moor Corp. • EMC 3717

North America

©2005 by Evan-Moor Corp. • EMC 3717

North America

©2005 by Evan-Moor Corp. • EMC 3717

North America

©2005 by Evan-Moor Corp. • EMC 3717

North America

©2005 by Evan-Moor Corp. • EMC 3717

Answer Key

North America

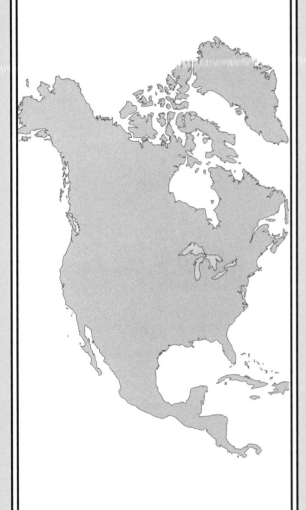

Lift the flap to check your answers.

North America

Part 1

Question	Answer
1.	D
2.	F
3.	C
4.	E
5.	A
6.	B

Part 2

1. Canada
2. United States
3. Mexico

North America

©2005 by Evan-Moor Corp. • EMC 3717

North America

©2005 by Evan-Moor Corp. • EMC 3717